RESISTANCE AND CONTEMPLATION

Paul Campbell

James W. Douglass

RESISTANCE AND CONTEMPLATION

The Way of Liberation

A DELTA BOOK

For Dan and Phil who showed the way
For Shelley who lit it with love and hope
And thanks to you, Tom Merton

Contents

Preface

This book began with the lives of certain people, and has been written in response to them.

One beginning was Phil and Dan Berrigan, who bloodied and napalmed draft files and said that resistance is serious, the people are being murdered, resist with them and live through dying—do it through love. I clearly remember opening a newspaper one morning on the University of Hawaii campus, reading of the Catonsville Nine, and feeling the shock of those thoughts. *Resistance and Contemplation* is an effort to hear more deeply Dan's and Phil's good news of resistance, and is therefore dedicated to them.

Another beginning was Thomas Merton. While teaching one year in Louisville, Kentucky, I lived not far from the Abbey of Gethsemani and visited Merton at his hermitage in the woods. It was early in 1965 and the war in Vietnam was coming home, though few really knew it. Merton knew it in his hermitage. He also knew that racism was stuck in the heart of America, when everyone else was singing "We Shall Overcome." Tom Merton prayed, listened, and wrote furious essays against the powers of destruction which he glimpsed first of all in himself. Merton seemed to know the way as no one else did. He took joy in it. At the hermitage he shared that way and joy, and without saying much, showed the roots of resistance. Since his death, I've read Merton more carefully in an effort to understand the roots.

A third beginning has been Shelley, my wife, who has taught me more deeply than even Merton and the Berrigans what the contemplative dimension of resistance means. She once wrote me, at a time when our lives were powerless to meet each other, "We must be strong in our acceptance of impotence before we'll be given any real Power." The book is an impossible effort to translate that way of truth and love mediated for me by Shelley into words which can somehow mediate it once again for others. Shelley's and my life together has been the experiential resource corresponding to Tom Merton's writings.

There have been other beginnings, the most significant having come from the members of the Hawaii Resistance. One occurred the afternoon Wayne Hayashi came in late to our University of Hawaii seminar on "The Theology of Peace" and told me the course finally made sense: he'd just burned his draft card (with eleven other students, the nucleus of the Hawaii Resistance). The course made sense for me, the professor, three months later, when Wayne and I were in jail together for sitting in front of a troop convoy (but an action taken only after I had argued until dawn the morning before at a Resistance meeting against civil disobedience—then finally becoming aware on the street that it was Resistance leader John Witeck who was right instead, and sitting with John, Wayne, and other resisters while the police motorcycles bore down on us).

I wish to dedicate Part II of this book, "The Way," to the members of the Hawaii Resistance 1968–70, and in particular Dana Park, Nick Reidy, Richard Tanimura, Butch Drury, Gary Gray, Tom Met, and Rich Walker, who endured prison and exile for the sake of liberation.

A number of friends read carefully and criticized for me the chapters of the book. I am grateful to them: Bob Aitken, Dave Burrell, Ned Butler, Richard de la Chaumiere, Chris Cotter, John Cox, Chuck Darst, Jim Forest, Jim Holloway, Phil Kelly, Julius Lester, Ian Lind, Mike McKale, Pat McNulty, Ben Norris, Basil O'Leary. I am especially grateful to Chuck Giuli, who from a nut farm on the Big Island was the first to say yin-yang and has been yin-yanging his way through the manuscript ever since.

Mary Carbray is the greatest Seattle librarian a Hedley, B.C., writer ever had helping him. Thank you, Mary.

It has always been a joy to work with Elizabeth Bartelme, my editor, whose faith in the book from the beginning made this year writing it possible.

James W. Douglass

Hedley, British Columbia
August 17, 1971.

Part One: Yin - Yang

What is the life of the guerrilla fighter like?
His normal life is the long hike.

Che Guevara

One thing seems sure; the new man will not spring
from Jove's forehead. The gods, the true gods of
man's history, of his worship, do not work miracles
of debased magic, on behalf of the morally indolent.
No; such a man will get born because he has trodden
the furnace, and died there.

Daniel Berrigan

What is night for all beings is the time of waking
for the disciplined soul.

The *Bhagavad-Gita*

A way of liberation passes through fire.

In September 1953 a New York businessman named Philip Kapleau quit his business, sold his possessions, said good-bye to friends who questioned his sanity, and moved to Japan where he entered a Zen monastery. Kapleau had decided to turn his philosophical interest in Zen into a personal quest for liberation, and in Japan he placed himself under the discipline of Zen masters, or *roshis,* so as to seek the profoundly unifying experience of Zen known as *satori.* Kapleau then struggled for years to master in mind and body the way to liberation: rising at 3:30 A.M., meditating cross-legged much of the day and into the night, legs aching and body shivering through long winters in the unheated *zendo;* living on a rice diet obtained by begging with his fellow monks; all the while, under the demanding direction of his roshi, concentrating ever more intensely on the Zen formulation, or *koan,* which once penetrated would grant him the experience of ultimate Truth.

After five years of striving in this way, Kapleau, like thousands of Zen students before him, sat one day before his roshi and listened to a familiar teaching which exploded through the final barriers within him and gave him the experience of liberation:

> "The universe is One," [the roshi] began, each word tearing into my mind like a bullet. "The moon of Truth—"
> All at once the roshi, the room, every single thing disappeared in a dazzling stream of illumination and I felt myself bathed in a delicious, unspeakable delight . . . For a fleeting eternity I was alone—I alone was . . . Then the roshi swam into view. Our eyes met and flowed into each other, and we burst out laughing . . .[1]

A way of liberation passes through fire, in Kapleau's case the fire of an inner spiritual discipline. In a dialogue with D. T. Suzuki, Thomas Merton identified the purifying fire of Zen liberation as the angel's flaming sword placed by God in front of the Garden of Eden, "to guard the way to the tree of life" after Adam's sin. The flaming sword does not mean that the freedom of paradise, which is the Gospel's "purity of heart," is no longer possible after man has left it, but only that recovering it is a matter of great practical difficulty. As St. Ambrose puts it: "All who wish to return to paradise must be tested by the fire." Merton adds:

> The way from knowledge to innocence, or the purification of the heart, is a way of temptation and struggle. It is a matter of wrestling with supreme difficulties and overcoming obstacles that seem, and indeed are, beyond human strength.[2]

Recovering that profound inner freedom of Zen which is the experience of paradise, in a realization of the unity of existence, requires that the seeker walk a narrow way

[1] Philip Kapleau, ed., *The Three Pillars of Zen* (Beacon Press: 1967), p. 228.
[2] Thomas Merton, *Zen and the Birds of Appetite* (New Directions: 1968), pp. 123–24.

on which he will feel the angel's flaming sword of liberation descend on his self.

Another way of liberation passes through fire:

On November 25, 1956, at two in the morning, a band of revolutionaries led by Fidel Castro pushed off in a boat from the coast of Mexico and headed for Cuba, not far ahead of agents from three governments seeking their arrest or execution. After seven days of hunger and seasickness on their poorly equipped boat, Castro and his men landed on a Cuban beach, were spotted by a coast guard cutter, and in great haste entered the cover of a swamp where they were bombed by enemy planes. For three days they marched, until overcome by extreme sickness and exhaustion. Then while resting at the edge of a cane field, they were ambushed by a large number of Batista's troops. The revolutionary force was thereby reduced from eighty-two men to twelve (including a badly wounded Che Guevara), who managed to survive the attack and flee in several groups to the Sierra Maestra Mountains— where after several weeks of narrowly evading government troops, they would regroup and begin a series of guerrilla counter-attacks that would lead eventually to Cuba's liberation.

A way of liberation passes through fire, in this case the fire of revolutionary discipline met by overwhelming force. History's price for the people's liberation from oppression is the blood of those willing to seek that liberation with their entire lives. To speak of the people's liberation is to speak of such lives—the lives of Fidel Castro, Che Guevara, Camilo Torres—in which belief was made flesh in action and in a struggle with the powers of oppression to the point of suffering love and death. Che Guevara emphasized this sacrificial love: ". . . the true revolutionary is moved by strong feelings of love. It is impossible to conceive of an authentic revolutionary who lacks this quality."[3]

Camilo Torres, the Catholic priest who was killed with the Colombian guerrillas he joined, once explained to Colombian students what sacrifices were demanded in the struggle for liberation:

> It is essential that the revolutionary conviction of each student be so ingrained that he accept it in its totality, even to the ultimate consequences. Poverty and persecution must not be sought after. But, given the present situation, they are the logical consequences of a battle to the end against the existing structures. Under the present system, they are the signs which give authenticity to a revolutionary life.[4]

Torres' words should remind us that it is these same signs, poverty and persecution, which are cited by Jesus as a means of identifying the followers of his way.

Liberation has two dimensions: freedom from the bondage of the individual self, as in Zen, and freedom from the extended self of social oppression, as in liberation movements in Latin America and Southeast Asia. Neither dimension of freedom, personal or social, can be won without suffering. We begin always on the

[3] Che Guevara, *Socialism and Man in Cuba*. Quoted on the front cover of his *Reminiscences of the Cuban Revolutionary War* (Grove Press: 1968).

[4] John Alvarez Garcia and Christian Restrepo Calle, eds., *Camilo Torres: His Life and His Message*, translated by Virginia M. O'Grady (Templegate Publishers: 1968), p. 99.

far side of the flaming sword, the purifying fire of
revolutionary suffering. I am bound to the wheel of
my self. At the same time my brothers and sisters
and I are bound to the wheel of exploitation and war. To
reach liberation I strain to move the wheel of bondage
under one guise or the other, and the wheel I choose rolls
into the flame of truth. Perhaps then, if my commitment
can endure the fire, I realize a dimension of freedom.
Even so, I am troubled as I feel my continuing bondage
to the other wheel.

But consider the possibility of a further experiment
in truth. Join the two wheels of bondage, and with
yourself on the rim, roll them as one into the fire of
truth. Seek liberation into a freedom where the two
dimensions would combine in one explosive whole. Pass
into a fire whose intensity is one with Reality Itself.

Thus did a Vietnamese woman live and act.

In the first months of 1967, the people of South Vietnam were living in an atmosphere which even in their
oppressive history was an unusually suffocating one. In
the eyes of the American people, South Vietnam was
in the process of becoming a constitutional democracy.
The Ky-Thieu government had apparently approved
and organized elections, the first of which (for a
Constituent Assembly to write a constitution) had already taken place in September 1966. These elections
were being widely publicized by the American government as proof of South Vietnam's democratic process.
In fact, however, as the Vietnamese were intensely aware,
the leading peace candidates opposing the government
had all been jailed before the elections, and as a
further safeguard, all "unreliable" citizens were charged

with being Communists by the regime and denied reg-
istration. Moreover, the fraudulent elections occurred
shortly after a powerful Buddhist-led uprising in Hue
had almost toppled the regime before it was overcome
by Ky's tanks flown in by American planes. Thus as
1967 began, the most recent hopes of the Vietnamese
lay crushed by American weapons and silenced in
the prisons of a police state, while the American government and press told the world jubilantly of the
expansion of democracy in South Vietnam.

In this atmosphere, on May 16, 1967, a young woman
named Nhat Chi Mai, who was a student and social
worker known for her tireless service to the people, invited some of her friends to meet her on the steps of
the Tu Nghiem Pagoda in Saigon. When her friends
arrived, Nhat Chi Mai was sitting in the lotus position
facing two statues, one of the Virgin Mary, the other
of the (Mother) Bodhisattva Quan Am. She had with
her a basin, which her friends assumed was for the
ceremony of "washing the Buddha." In fact the basin
was filled with gasoline, which Nhat Chi Mai poured
over herself. Only when she ignited herself did they
realize what was happening. As the flames consumed
her, Nhat Chi Mai remained fixed in an attitude of
prayer until she was dead. Between the two statues in
front of her, she had placed a strip of cloth on which
she had written:

> I wish to use my body as a torch
> to dissipate the darkness
> to waken Love among men
> and to bring peace to Vietnam

Nhat Chi Mai had left other messages and poems
with friends, including pleas to all Vietnamese to stop

murdering one another, and one to President Johnson to stop the war. She wrote to her fellow countrymen:

> In order that my love for all and my aspiration for Peace not be misunderstood or deliberately distorted,
> I AM BURNING MYSELF
> asserting that my sacrifice is for *Peace in Vietnam* and for *Love and Justice*.
>
> I pray that the flame that is consuming my body will burn away all ambition and hatred which have been pushing many of us into the Hell of the Soul and creating so much suffering among human beings.
>
> I pray that the human race will be able to inherit Buddha's Compassion, Jesus' Love and the legacy of man's humaneness.

She wrote to President Johnson:

> The more you escalate the war, the more you intensify your efforts here, the greater defeat you will get. Because of your mistakes, you are now without a right cause. Please re-read Vietnamese history.[5]

She signed her name below the words, "Respectfully, the one who burns herself to oppose War."

The day after Nhat Chi Mai's death, all of Saigon's newspapers had blank spaces where news of the immolation had been censored by the government. Even the family's announcement of the death had been taken out. Nevertheless news of Nhat Chi Mai's sacrifice spread quickly among the people, and their response was such that her funeral procession, two days later, filled Saigon's streets with so many participants that it became a peace march which took five hours to pass a single point.

[5] The poems and messages of Nhat Chi Mai are printed as an appendix in Alfred Hassler's *Saigon, U.S.A.* (Richard W. Baron: 1970), pp. 199–204, under the title *"The Poems of Phan Thi Mai."* I have drawn the details of her life and death from Hassler, pp. 105, 135, from the news bulletin of the Vietnamese Peace Delegation to Paris, and from *Lotus,* a Vietnamese newsletter published in the United States.

What is the meaning of Nhat Chi Mai's self-immolation? A venerated Buddhist monk and poet, Thich Nhat Hanh, has described it as a manifestation of her "willingness to suffer for the sake of the enlightenment of the people. In its essence it does not differ from the act of Christ in his death on the Cross."[6]

The death of Nhat Chi Mai like the death of Jesus, a dying so that others might live, shows that the inner freedom of Zen—or the "purity of heart" of the Gospel—is not the ultimate end of liberation. The enlightenment of a pure heart which Philip Kapleau realized in the presence of his *roshi* is a profoundly important stage on the way to liberation. But in a world of mass injustice and murder, such enlightenment is only *a* stage —and unless left behind, will become a prison itself. Unless the experience of enlightenment can be realized anew in direct relation to the bondage of all the people, on that plane of struggle where the Cuban revolutionaries gave their lives (but without recourse to Zen), freedom will have become its own end in one's private psyche while other members of the human family suffer and die unaided.

The liberating power of Nhat Chi Mai is in Buddhist terms the ideal of the *bodhisattva,* the enlightened being whose great compassion moves her to go beyond her own enlightenment and dedicate herself to helping all other creatures attain liberation. Thich Nhat Hanh's reference to Christ on the cross is at this point precise in both Buddhist and Christian terms, for the bodhisattva ideal of self-sacrifice for the sake of others lost in darkness could have been realized no more per-

[6] Thich Nhat Hanh, *Love in Action: The Non-Violent Struggle for Peace in Vietnam* (distributed by the Overseas Vietnamese Buddhists Association, June 1969), p. 12.

fectly than by One who out of love for humanity emptied himself, taking the form of a servant, and died for the ultimate union of all. It was therefore in complete understanding that Nhat Chi Mai placed before her in her act of self-sacrifice the statues of the Mother Bodhisattva and the Mother of Christ, who brought together for a Vietnamese woman the Buddha's compassion and Jesus' love. The torch which Nhat Chi Mai became was a torch of enlightenment for the people, in the sense of Buddhism, at the same time as it was a realization of the kingdom and a light for all the world, in the sense of the Gospel.

Within this context of Buddhist and Christian belief, it should also be said, however, that a fundamental reason why Nhat Chi Mai's sacrificial act had such power and significance is that it was done in Vietnam, in specific relation to an eighteen-hundred-year-old Buddhist tradition and to a more modern Catholicism which has nevertheless begun, in the lives of some radical Vietnamese Catholics, to de-Westernize itself and to absorb Vietnamese ways of thought and action. The symbolic power of Nhat Chi Mai was therefore a power of Vietnam, drawing on a spiritual and cultural heritage which no citizen of the West has at his or her command for the simple reason that, however much the Westerner may wish to identify with such a heritage, the Vietnamese are not in fact his people, and their history not his history. The power of such action, nonviolent and sacrificial in character, is a symbolic power to engage the heart and mind of one's people, through the specific history and culture in which they have been formed. Nhat Chi Mai's self-immolation made spiritual and cultural sense in Vietnam, and moved her peo-

ple, in a way that it could not conceivably have done
in any Western country. This is to say that a Western,
and particularly an American, admirer of this Vietnamese saint would have to look to his own history to
decide on forms of action which would speak to his
own people—as non-violent leaders such as Cesar Chavez
and Daniel and Philip Berrigan have in fact done.

In Vietnam Mai's action could be felt among Catholics as well as Buddhists, as she intended by her choice
of symbols. Father Nguyen Ngoc Lan, an intellectual
leader of Vietnamese Catholics, undertook the task of
publishing Nhat Chi Mai's poems and letters, in spite
of the ban placed upon them by the Saigon government. More than a hundred thousand copies were
circulated. In his foreword to the book, Father Lan
asked: if Mai after dying so she could speak, could
not, after all, speak, "Who among the living would dare
to speak then? And who to listen?"[7]

The people listened to Mai and understood her
death as a sacrifice offered for them, "to dissipate the
darkness." In May 1971, on the fourth anniversary of
her immolation, thirty associations representing virtually
every aspect of Vietnamese society held a religious ceremony in the pagoda where Nhat Chi Mai had sacrificed
herself, to rededicate themselves to the realization of her
purpose. A crowd numbering tens of thousands thronged
in and around the pagoda. The significance of this
ceremony had not been lost to the Saigon government.
Observers of the scene reported that the largest army
of police ever seen in Saigon, armed with fixed bayonets
and tear-gas grenades, tried to block the streets leading to the pagoda. But the people streamed by without

[7] Quoted in *Lotus*.

provoking the police, and were able to hear the leading members of their society (those not already in jail) recommit themselves to the struggle for peace and justice in Vietnam.

A way of liberation passes through fire because the only God who has been known to liberate is the God who continually suffers and dies in humanity out of love for the people. Liberation is the fruit of crucifixion. Easter follows Good Friday, and the resurrection of humanity the believing community's sacrifice of its own blood. The revolution is won by the giving of lives. To speak of liberation is therefore to speak of such lives, but our evocation of their life has power only if we are able to speak finally with the witness of our own lives. Our talk of liberation becomes serious when we realize sharply that we are saved by the liberator's blood only when we allow it to mix with our own. "Can you drink the cup that I must drink, or be baptized with the baptism with which I must be baptized?" The disciples said, "We can," and the God of History took them seriously.

After entering prison for a six-year sentence for destroying draft records, Father Philip Berrigan spoke to the point: "Life is more precious than liberty, and to offer up one's life is more difficult than to surrender one's property. But my conscience did not allow self-immolation, so I gave what was possible."[8] To Berrigan's understanding of what liberation demands, a six-year sentence was getting off lightly. Phil Berrigan is alive today only because his conscience would not allow self-

[8] Philip Berrigan, *Prison Journals of a Priest Revolutionary* (Holt, Rinehart and Winston: 1970), p. 109.

immolation. And he realized his freedom in prison because he recognized in conscience and in act that the price of liberation is a man's whole life.

A way of liberation passes through fire. The first question, then, which a way of liberation raises is: To what extent am I willing to pass through that fire myself?

A second question has to do with the social and global dimension of a way of liberation: How shall we understand more precisely that plane of freedom's struggle, that dimension of seeking liberation, which has been represented by Fidel Castro and Che Guevara in terms of guerrilla warfare? Assuming for a moment the commitment to the people of the compassionate bodhisattva and the self-emptying Christ, what today is the nature of the common bondage to which they must respond?

A fact of our history demands recognition first. In most parts of the world today, most obviously in Vietnam but no less murderously in Latin America, the liberator's blood is being shed in resistance to the United States of America, and specifically in resistance to its policy of forcibly managing the economies of other states and peoples. The fact with which contemporary liberation movements have to contend is the fact of United States imperialism and its consequences in the lives of hundreds of millions of people, most of them living in the Southern Hemisphere. I think that Carl Oglesby's analysis of that fact is accurate and morally devastating:

> There is nothing more common in our economic mentality, nothing more constant in our foreign policy, than this conviction that the basic problem of the American business system is domestically undistributable wealth, and that the basic solution to that problem, its essential and only anodyne, lies in our penetration of

foreign markets—most especially, the markets of those lands which we now think of as the under-developed (or in the new State Department tact, the *less*-developed) countries.

. . . For us, peace finally exists when the world is finally safe for American businessmen to carry on their business everywhere, on terms as favorable as they can be made, in settings managed preferably by native middle-class governments, but if need be by oligarchic and repressive ones, by the old foreign grads of Fort Bragg, or if the panic hits in a pivotal place, by our own Marines.[9]

If the compassion of the Buddha is real, if Christ's love for the human family is to be present, then love must seek and find a way to free humanity from a system of wealth and power in which 6 per cent of the world's people, Americans, own 60 per cent of the world's wealth.

Love must discover a way of liberation from what Felix Greene has described as the assumption (at the very heart of capitalism) that "it is normal, natural and right for individuals of one class to reap their wealth at the expense of those who actually produce the wealth."[10]

Love must discover a way to free the world from 3,401 military bases which the United States operates overseas as the means of repressing any challenge to her wealth and power.[11]

Love must discover a way for Americans to begin to understand what it has meant in people's lives for the

[9] Carl Oglesby and Richard Shaull, *Containment and Change* (Macmillan paperback: 1967), pp. 65–66, 70–71.

[10] Felix Greene, *The Enemy: What Every American Should Know About Imperialism* (Vintage: 1971), p. 102.

[11] The number of U.S. overseas bases was published in a New York *Times* dispatch dated April 9, 1969, and quoted at length in Greene, pp. 225–26.

United States to have spent $1,000 *billion* on its military establishment since World War II, a fraction of which could have rebuilt every slum in the country.

Love must discover a way to revolutionize the American economy so that it is no longer dependent on war and on adding more weapons to the most incredibly destructive arsenal the world has ever known.

Love must discover a way to liberate humanity from the system of exploitation and oppression which at this moment of history is embodied primarily, though by no means exclusively, in the political, economic, and military empire of the United States.

And love *will* find a way to liberate humanity from this empire, for both history and the prophets tell us that the God of Love will not tolerate much longer what Americans envision forever—the endurance of a prosperity built on the lives of the world's poor. The relevant text of the Book of Revelation can be given a contemporary reading:

> Then a powerful angel picked up a boulder like a great millstone, and as he hurled it into the sea, he said, "That is how the great nation of America is going to be hurled down, never to be seen again.
>
> "Never again in you, America,
> will be be heard the song of bankers and generals,
> the music of drum and bugle marching abroad;
> never again will technicians of every skill be found
> or the sound of great industries be heard;
> never again will shine the light of the frontier,
> never again will be heard
> the voices of explorers and traders.
> Your corporate heads were the princes of the earth,
> all the nations were under your spell.
>
> In America you will find the blood of prophets and saints." (Revelation 18:21-24)

The crimes of the greatest military and economic empire in history make the Apocalypse an even more living prophecy in our day than it was to the embattled Christians of the first century. This is the kind of empire with which liberation movements have to deal now, an empire beginning to be drunk on the blood of prophets and saints. A way of liberation must pass through the fire of this empire's power, but those who travel the way can take strength in the vision of a new humanity at the end and the fate of all murderous powers under the final rule of the Lamb who was slain.

If the prophets envision the destruction of imperial power and the liberation of all oppressed peoples in a new heaven and a new earth, they leave to each generation of believers the task of embodying that struggle and of moving humanity from here to there in the grace of the Lord. The end is certain. The exploiters will fall from power, and the poor will inherit the earth. In that important respect Marx borrowed his vision from Jesus. But even given the faith to hold to an eschatological vision, we also know that liberation occurs in stages, and we need to understand more of its form within history, and in our own time in particular.

In terms of the Gospel, the history of man's liberation from injustice is an outward aspect of the inward growth of man into God. Liberation is the consequence of God's explosion of love in history, made visible in the cross of Jesus of Nazareth. Liberation is the political expression of humanity's transformation in love. It becomes possible whenever man turns from the will to power and instead acknowledges in his depths the power of Love. The growth of God's Love in man, and his transformation into the man-God, is the process which results finally in the breaking of chains and the freeing of slaves. The political liberation of humanity is a sign of God's redeeming presence breaking the bonds of sin.

This is a liberation which is achieved above all through non-violent struggle. The paradigm of liberation is the cross and the empty tomb, crucifixion and resurrection, suffering love and transforming power. Liberation is the redemption of man from his violence, a socially and personally pervasive violence, a violence that is both within and without. Liberation is the cross of self-emptying, suffering, and non-violent love which moves one to faith, and to a deeper humanity. Deeper even than any repossession of the land by the people is the renewal of their humanity in a struggle which is truthful, loving, and life-giving. Humanity needs that struggle even more than it needs a victorious end, for the struggle is the victory. Liberation is a struggle for the non-violent transformation of a society of oppression and fear into a community of love. It is a necessary, beautiful, impossible, eternal task, and is thus undertaken now in a self-crucifying, life-serving struggle which can be realized fully only at the end of history. Non-violence is that central means of liberation which is also its end in a new heaven and a new earth.

Nevertheless, the vision of faith cannot be withdrawn from a history in which God's liberating presence often takes more ambiguous forms than the cross of Jesus. Freedom is won in stages, and a liberating love may appear at one stage in the form of a paradox. This is true of our own history, in which a powerful sign of liberation has been the humanity of the National Liberation Front of Vietnam in its sustained resistance to an

overwhelming military power. I do not believe that the
NLF's means of resistance are liberating enough to hold
any hope for a world verging on nuclear self-destruction.
Nor can the members of the NLF with their weapons
begin to realize the ideal of the bodhisattva embodied
by the sacrifice of their sister, Nhat Chi Mai. But given
the conditions of their struggle, I believe not only
that the humanity of the NLF goes much deeper than
its opponents in the Pentagon, but that in its toughness,
faith, endurance, and imagination, the NLF can serve
as a cutting edge today for the requirements of non-
violent liberation. Believers in non-violence can learn
from the humanity and lessons of the NLF.[12]

One such lesson of the NLF, a lesson from history
which needs to be constantly reseen in the light of the
Gospel's stress on poverty, is that a liberation movement
will always derive its spirit and its strength from the
bottom of a social structure. The enigma of the war
in Vietnam for the American mind, once it realized the
disproportionate wealth and firepower of the opposing
forces, has been: What is holding up the "Viet Cong"?
The beginning of an answer can be found simply in
poverty. The strength of the NLF is the strength of the
Vietnamese poor. There is no technological equivalent,
however great one's bombing capacity, for a human
being who has been truly disciplined by poverty and
who has accepted suffering and the expectancy of early

---

[12] Two first-hand and largely sympathetic portraits of the National
Liberation Front are Wilfred G. Burchett, *Vietnam: Inside Story of the
Guerilla War* (New World Paperbacks: 1965) and Katsuichi Honda, *The
National Liberation Front* (printed in Japan, 1968). Douglas Pike is
sharply critical of the NLF in his two books *Viet Cong* (The M.I.T.
Press: 1966) and *War, Peace, and the Viet Cong* (The M.I.T. Press:
1969), which are based on NLF documents obtained by the U. S. In-
formation Agency.

death as a way of life. The man who has learned for
years to live without comfort and without hope of a
future will be prepared to tunnel beneath jungle floors
or lie motionless in rice paddies, enduring the endless
firepower and surfacing to fight back furiously whenever the enemy shows a weakness. In the jungles of
Indochina, the discipline of the poor has proved to be
more than a counter to the firepower of Western technicians.

To go a notch deeper on an understanding of the
NLF, the poverty and suffering of its members are shared
and sustained by a larger community. Their struggle is
a people's struggle, and the people give them strength
—not only the material aid necessary to continue a guerrilla struggle, but fundamental to that, a sense of solidarity with the history, dignity, and destiny of a whole
people. The Vietnamese resistance is an expression of
the people's will to determine the future of their own
country and repel foreign invaders. Thus its basic power
has not been ideological but human, grassroots, decen-
tralized, and in many ways instinctive.

But the final answer to the enigma of the NLF's neu-
tralizing American might is that the NLF is strong
because it is planted in the truth. If there has ever been
a war in which the power of truth was clearly dominant
on one side, it is the war between the Pentagon and
the peasants of Vietnam. The President of the National
Liberation Front was once asked if the coming of a
military specialist like Maxwell Taylor, with the enormous power at his disposal, hadn't heightened the prospect of American victory. He replied:

> The fact is that the defeats since Maxwell Taylor came
> here have been greater, more important than the disasters

before he arrived. I would like to add that this is not the fault of Taylor. It is the fault of a war of aggression, an unjust war. It is not a question of sending top-rank strategists; not a question of highly-trained troops and ultra-modern arms in a war of this type. Of course the relation of forces is decisive, but these are not only material forces. Above all it is morale that counts; it is the human factor that is decisive. If one could take into account only material forces we would have been crushed long ago, given the enormous disproportion. In fact it is they who are being crushed. No Maxwell Taylors can change that.[13]

Not even the greatest military power in man's history is capable of "winning the minds and hearts of the people," or to put it less obliquely, is capable of emptying their souls of the truth of their resistance. Given the most decisive task of the Indochina war, that of embodying the truth, United States power has been impotent. The Vietnamese know, and they know that we know, whose land it is and where justice lies. And they embody their belief that the truth will make them free.

The NLF is strong in poverty, community, and the truth, strong enough to have resisted to a standoff a military Goliath. Why then not follow the tendency of the Left today to adopt uncritically the NLF's central method of guerrilla violence as a universal pattern for liberation movements, whether in Asia or the Americas? Why choose non-violence in contrast to a liberation movement apparently effective in other terms?

In spite of the real lessons of the NLF, there is first of all a deep contradiction, and secondly, an enormous danger in its pattern of resistance. The truth which will make humanity free must not only be struggled for at the expense of one's life. It must also be embodied fully

13 Burchett, p. 240.

in the most human and loving means possible if it is to reach other men and women holding contrary positions. However great the pressures arguing for violence, a gun remains a very imperfect means of defending or serving the truth, and the truth is inevitably compromised and obscured by its use. It is the truth of their cause which NLF leaders have recognized as the basis of their strength. But that truth of the NLF is contradicted by a violence which takes the lives of other Vietnamese and Americans, most of them also victims of imperialism, and who cannot recognize a truth which denies them life.

Millions of Vietnamese have been injured or killed, millions more uprooted, and a country laid waste in a violent liberation struggle. Had the NLF's degree of commitment been given to a non-violent struggle for the same truth, I believe that truth would have had a more liberating effect upon Vietnam, the United States, and the world, without resulting in such indescribable suffering for the Vietnamese people. The truth of the cause of Vietnamese peasants has been compromised by involvement in a power struggle between the world's two ideological camps.

A tragic consequence of the NLF's courageous but truth-contradicting struggle is that a deeply committed non-violent movement having largely the same aims has in fact arisen in Vietnam, only to be submerged in the bitter fighting and ideological noise between the United States-Saigon and Hanoi-NLF forces. It is this movement, centered on the Buddhist Church and led by a young Buddhist monk, Thich Tri Quang, which was represented by Nhat Chi Mai in her sacrifice and which accounts for the size and depth of the people's response to her.

It is a movement which has overthrown two Saigon dictatorships, Diem's in 1963 and General Khanh's in 1964, only to be frustrated in each case by military coups backed by the United States embassy and CIA which returned a police state to power. This movement would have likely brought down the Ky-Thieu government as well, in 1966, had not the United States responded to Ky's plight by flying his forces into the center of the "struggle movement" in Hue, and by withholding supplies, including vitally needed gasoline, from those troops which were defecting from him. In January 1969 the struggle movement mounted a peace demonstration in Saigon which involved an estimated 500,000 participants, in the capital city of a country where even speaking for peace is a crime.[14]

But little is known in the West of this non-violent movement, in spite of its size and power in South Vietnam, which according to a number of observers exceeds that of the NLF. For the United States government and press acknowledge only North Vietnam and the NLF as the Saigon government's opposition. Thus the armed conflict with its ideological echoes in Paris obscures the non-violent struggle for peace and independence, conveniently so for Washington and Saigon, which are more comfortable fighting Communist guerrillas than Buddhist monks.

A closer look therefore at the conflict in Vietnam gives one reason to qualify "the lesson of the NLF" by reservations regarding both its choice of means and its exclusive claims to being the people's alternative to Saigon. The

[14] Hassler writes extensively on the Buddhist movement in *Saigon, U.S.A.* Its spokesman is Thich Nhat Hanh; see his *Vietnam: Lotus in a Sea of Fire* (Hill and Wang: 1967).

genuine truth and humanity of the NLF's struggle is contradicted by its violence, which prevents other men from recognizing its truth, and by its ideology and propaganda, which stand in contrast to the Buddhists' ability to combine an openness to all truth with a commitment to liberation at least as great as the Front's.[15]

Besides its contradiction to a liberating truth, the enormous danger of guerrilla violence is that it will provoke genocide. When a liberation movement chooses violence, it engages in a form of conflict whose most murderous possibilities are controlled by the imperial power's choice of weapons. Or a second possibility as the liberation movement increases in power: It places itself under the nuclear wing of the Soviet Union or China, as Cuba did with the former in 1962. It is difficult to imagine a more fundamental moral contradiction than the spectacle of a liberation leader (Fidel Castro in '62) surrendering the fate of his country and the world to the nuclear power struggle between a left-wing and a right-wing imperialism. Yet the contradiction is implicit in the guerrilla's choice of violence as his way of liberation from imperialism. The only real long-range alternative to genocide and a global holocaust,

[15] Yet both the Front and the Buddhists receive the support of the people. Their attitude is suggested by the remark of a Saigon University student to Hassler (p. 160): "You see, when you Americans ask how many Vietnamese support the Buddhists and how many support the Front, you begin with a misunderstanding. There is not that kind of division. At the top, perhaps, yes. Leaders of both groups understand well what their differences are and where their allegiances lie. But as soon as you get down into the population, the sharp line vanishes. The same people support the Front because of its stand for independence and the Buddhists for their insistence on peace. Combine the two, create a government that demonstrates its independence—you understand that I mean independence from the foreigners, the Americans—and its commitment to peace, and no one could oppose it."

whose likelihood increases with the success of violent liberation, is the kind of radical shift in spirit which is the object of non-violent revolution. In order to realize a healing future, the world needs to be redeemed from war as well as racism and imperialism. Non-violent liberation responds equally to all those needs.

The truth of liberation needs to be taken on as a way of life, doubly so by a believer in non-violence. If the NLF with its violent contradictions can still exemplify a life steeled in poverty, community, and the truth, what are we Americans who profess non-violence in a far less oppressive context to think of our commitment? What value, for example, should we give to our periodical mass marches (with occasional civil disobedience) at those high points when the peace movement can reduce its in-fighting sufficiently to generate a new wave of action? What value alongside the suffering and dying in Vietnamese jungles, the routine torture of thousands of political resisters in Saigon jails?

A story can illustrate contrasting styles of non-violence. Early in 1967 Alfred Hassler, executive director of the Fellowship of Reconciliation, a well-known American peace organization, made a trip to Saigon in order to confer secretly with members of the Vietnamese struggle movement. One night he met with several leaders of the student underground peace movement, who told him of their plan to shock the American people into realizing the agony of their country: Twenty of them were going to burn themselves to death at the same time on the steps of the University of Dalat.

Hassler, who had already gained great respect for the courage and dedication of these students, who were constantly pursued by the Saigon police, pleaded with them not to carry out their plan. He proposed an alternative way to reach the American people. One hundred American student leaders had recently addressed a letter to President Johnson protesting the war. Why did not the Vietnamese students, who were their counterparts, address a letter in turn to these American students thanking them for their action and pleading with them for additional understanding and help?

The Vietnamese students agreed to Hassler's proposal. A few nights later they gave him their statement to the Americans, which was illegal under South Vietnamese law and had been signed at great risk by fifty-nine student leaders and eleven faculty members.

When Hassler returned to New York City, he sent the Vietnamese students' plea, with an explanatory letter, by registered mail to each of the one hundred Americans. None of them replied. Not long after, Hassler was able to speak with twenty of these students at a meeting in New York. After listening to his further explanation of the background to the letter and the situation of the Vietnamese, during which they seemed moved, they sent him from the room while they discussed what they should do. Hassler describes their decision:

> Soon one of them came out to communicate their wish that I should write to the Vietnamese students and tell them how grateful for their peace efforts the Americans were, "but," he said, "without any publicity, please." He asked if we thought the Vietnamese would be pleased. No, we said, we did not, and asked why they wanted no publicity, and he explained that they did not wish to damage the credibility of their moderate position. They had just come from a meeting with Sec-

retary of State Dean Rusk, and thought they were having an effect on him.[16]

Six weeks later, Nhat Chi Mai, one of the Vietnamese students who had signed the statement, burned herself to death.

From the Vietnamese, jungle fighters and Buddhist resisters alike, we learn that liberation demands whole lives—and as a way of organizing resistance among the people, the giving of such lives as a statement of what the revolution is.

Liberation comes from the bottom of a society, from the kind of organizing which will express simply, directly, and militantly the needs and hopes of the poor. A good example of the spiritual-political power possible through such organizing is the success of Cesar Chavez and the United Farm Workers Organizing Committee in the grape strike and international grape boycott. Chavez' organizing began with painstaking investigations into local labor conditions, with a gathering of farm workers' own views on the changes they most needed, and with the building up of an enormous network of relationships of trust and common commitment. It was an organization built really on Chavez' life. The base of organizing was the life of poverty which he had experienced with the workers from the beginning, and which organizers and workers continued to share as the union grew. Only out of the community thus formed and deepened through years of shared pain and struggle, guided by Chavez' spiritual discipline, was it possible to develop a union with grass-roots power and non-violent guerrilla instincts—and which in turn provided the foundation and inspiration for an expand-

[16] Hassler, p. 104.

ing boycott organization. Poverty, community, and the truth of an uncontradicted cause lie behind the strength of Chavez' organization, which in an interview he characterizes as a non-violent Viet Cong:

> "There has to be a real organization, a living organization, there has to be . . . people in motion, and they have to be disciplined." He laughed. "I don't mean, like, *marching*, I mean a trained instinct so that when the moment comes, we just turn around and *hit* it. That's real organization. If you organize for demonstration, all you have is demonstration. You must demonstrate, and then return right away to the real work. We're so flexible, yet there's so much discipline that we do things and don't even talk about them. We can go down the highway at eighty miles an hour and throw her into reverse gear and not even screech. For instance, we can be striking today, and tomorrow morning or a couple of days later we can move the effort into a boycott without missing a step. We have a motion and rhythm. That mobility makes a difference. It can be compared to a prize fight, where the whole idea is to be in balance so that however bad things get, you don't get knocked out, and you're always ready to take advantage of their mistakes. By instinct more than anything else, when we see them make a mistake we move right in, and this is true right down to the simplest striker on the picket line." He grinned. "That's why they call us the Vietcong —it's guerrilla warfare."[17]

Organizing from society's ground floor, a working with the people rather than for them, is equally characteristic of Danilo Dolci's movement for non-violent revolution in western Sicily. In an area where the Mafia has its deepest roots, and where centuries of fatalism have deepened the people's passivity in the face of misery, Dolci's

---

[17] Peter Matthiessen, *Sal Si Puedes: Cesar Chavez and the New American Revolution* (Random House: 1969), pp. 158–59.

center of development teams, by sharing the lives of the poor yet acting aggressively for change, has given new hope and courage to the people. Dolci's strikes, demonstrations, and prolonged fasts have brought the poverty of Sicily to the attention of the world, and have pressured and shamed the Italian government into the construction of an important new irrigation system. His uncompromising stand against the Mafia has greatly reduced its violent hold on the population. By exhortation but even more by the example of committed, sharing lives, the center has spread seeds of revolutionary change across the whole of Sicily.

At the beginning of an act of civil disobedience designed to bring pressure on authorities for the construction of another dam, the occupation of a piazza accompanied by a four-day fast, Dolci spoke in simple terms to the assembled people of the values underlying their struggle:

> We are here to be of service, to join together people of various political beliefs toward one common cause. We shall fast not to ridicule the police, not to be photographed. Ours is a position of reason that emphasizes the distinction between force and truth. By our nonviolent action we shall show that truth has its own strength. Ours is a strategy based on love, not hate, and should result in a chain reaction of discussion and insight.[18]

It is through non-violent action that the full strength of truth is expressed and felt. The power of truth is the power to convince a man, to change his mind and heart, to turn him in the direction of justice and

[18] Jerre Mangione, *A Passion for Sicilians: The World Around Danilo Dolci* (William Morrow: 1968), p. 84.

humanity. The power of the truth, in this case the truth of the people's need for work and sustenance, is confronted by the entrenched prejudice and self-interest of the privileged. But the Truth which Gandhi identified with God is not oblivious to such men's redemption. <u>Truth seeks the liberation of both sides, poor and wealthy, from the common bondage of an inhuman relationship</u>. Truth is not sentimental. It recognizes the depth of oppression and the enormity of the task, the lives which will be required, if oppression is to be overcome. For that very reason, truth cannot afford to be compromised in its full power by the untruth of violence. Truth's answer to the problem of a social injustice more profound than was anticipated—as is always the case—is not the contradiction to truth of violence but rather more commitment, more imagination, more aggressive action, more love, more suffering, more of our lives in the struggle—for the medium of truth's power is neither a proposition nor a gun but a more and more loving human life.

Such organizations as Chavez' and Dolci's, built up with the people and disciplined by the poverty they seek to remove from others, are the base for a society's liberation from injustice and inhumanity. From a base in the people a liberation movement can be mounted to engage an oppressive power with the weapons of truth, so that, in the words of Phil Berrigan, power will be "stalemated, shamed, and even excoriated in some instances, and condemned, and hopefully, reduced to impotence."[19] Yet this is a revolution different in character from the one advocated by Camilo Torres when he said that "the heart of a revolution" is "to take power

[19] Berrigan, p. 197.

away from the privileged minority and give it to the poor majority."[20] Non-violent liberation seeks the redemption of humanity from power itself, from all power *over* men, which is a power of domination and sin. The only power non-violent liberation seeks is a power *for* man —the power to serve, to care, to love, to build the earth into a city of brothers and sisters, after the example of the God who loved and served humanity to the point of making himself powerless. An oppressive power will be shocked, shamed, and made impotent by the power of truth—if there are men and women willing to live out that truth without reservation—but the nullifying of the master's power is itself nullified if the former slave then hastens to seize power. Gandhi was wise in his rejection of all offices, and Dolci shrewd in his avoidance of political alliances. They knew that the power of revolution, a permanent revolution, lay elsewhere, and that to rule over men—regardless of the mandate—would be inevitably to lose power through men. To the revolutionary of the Kingdom, liberation will mean finally the disappearance of all power over men in the new reality of the human family's communion with the God of Love. The Gospel suggests that the way to realize that vision is to live it now in its fullness.

A way of liberation discovered through the Gospel will have its roots and its power in an almost forgotten faith, a faith of crucifixion and resurrection, a faith of scandalous death and joyful life. Jesus was only one of thousands of Jewish revolutionaries executed on Roman crosses. At the time of his death, one needed faith to believe that anything good or joyful could come from a cross. The faith of the cross is no less a scandal today,

[20] Garcia and Calle, p. 73.

and no less powerful in giving strength to the few who take it seriously. Phil Berrigan once wrote from a jail cell:

> If I were the lowliest of draft resisters, buried anonymously in some federal prison, forgotten by everyone but parents and one or two friends, I would be contributing more to the building of peace than the most spectacular dove, who makes headlines and rallies supporters, and whose exhortations are heard with apprehension even in the halls of government. "Yet to shame the wise, God has chosen what the world counts folly, and to shame what is strong, God has chosen what the world counts weakness. He has chosen things low and contemptible, mere nothings, to overthrow the existing order. And so there is no place for human pride in the presence of God." (I Cor. 1:27–29)[21]

Liberation is finally the resurrection, which is celebrated here now by men and women who know in their lives the promise and the presence of the Spirit: "Happy are the poor in spirit . . . the gentle . . . those who mourn . . . those who hunger and thirst for what is right . . ." The non-violent revolutionary acts out his faith in a kingdom of the poor, and through the cross finds it given already in the Spirit. When brothers and sisters resist the powers of domination with love and with truth, their lives celebrate life with a passion which scandalizes the joyless holders of power: Why are they so happy? Won't someone please tell them it's a jail, that they don't have the keys and can't get out? Why don't they understand that they can't be that happy?

Peter Matthiessen in the closing pages of his great book, *Sal Si Puedes: Cedar Chavez and the New American Revolution*, describes a revolutionary celebrating hu-

---

21 Berrigan, pp. 109–10.

manity's liberation with the kind of clowning the resurrection deserves:

> I think often of the visit to the archdiocese on that
> summer day in San Francisco, and the way Cesar
> vanished into the cold modern house of God, so unlike
> the simple missions he prefers. An elevator must have
> rushed him to the top, because moments later there
> came a rapping from on high, and Cesar appeared in
> silhouette behind the panes, waving and beckoning from
> the silences of sun and glass like a man trapped against
> his will in Heaven. His dance of woe was a pantomime
> of man's fate, and this transcendental clowning, this im-
> possible gaiety, which illuminates even his most desper-
> ate moments, is his most moving trait. Months later I
> could still see that human figure in the glittering high
> windows of the twentieth century. The hands, the dance,
> cried to the world: Wait! Have faith! Look, look! Let's
> go! Good-bye! Hello! I love you![22]

Yet as the rest of Chavez' life testifies, there is no
vision of resurrection which is not also a personal invitation to the cross.

This search for a way of liberation can end with the
reality and the question with which it began: A way of
liberation passes through fire. To what extent am I willing
to pass through that fire myself?

[22] Matthiessen, pp. 335-36.

THE YIN-YANG OF RESISTANCE AND CONTEMPLATION

On the back cover of his album *John Wesley Harding*, Bob Dylan has written a comment on man's willingness to pursue the truth. It offers a good introduction to the way of truth which is the first and last concern of this essay: the way of liberation. According to Dylan's oblique parable, three kings decided that a man named "Frank" was the key to understanding the new Dylan record (rather than "faith" or "froth," referring to two of the approaches of listeners anxious to pigeonhole the meaning of Dylan's music). The three kings crawled into Frank's room to see if he could help them. Frank acknowledged to the first king that he was indeed the key to understanding the record.

> "Well then," said the king in a bit of excitement, "could you please open it up for us?" Frank, who all this time had been reclining with his eyes closed, suddenly opened them both up as wide as a tiger. "And just how far would you like to go in?" he asked and the three kings all looked at each other. "Not too far but just far enough so's we can say that we've been there," said the first chief.

The parable is Dylan's way of commenting on the Magi, the followers of the star, who come seeking the latest revelation of truth from the artist they want to deify and identify with, without having recognized the seriousness and personal demand of truth in their own lives. It recalls Gandhi's statement, to those ready to canonize his every word yet unwilling to recognize the word in themselves, that he didn't want any followers, just people seriously pursuing their own truth, which would in the end bring all people together.

The point here is the same, as applied to the anxiety of all relevant Americans to identify ourselves with the oppressed—and in particular their media-inflated leaders —in their struggle for liberation. Our instincts tell us, as they should, that our liberation is somehow linked with the struggle of the oppressed, and we crawl into the presence of liberation leaders (captured dead or alive on videotape and lecture tours) seeking their truth. But the existential response, when reality breaks in, is the same chilling question of truth:

Just how far would we like to go in? Just how far would we like to go into the reality of liberation, given a recognition that real liberation can be entered only through the blood of people's lives—the lives of Nhat Chi Mai, Malcolm X, Martin Luther King, Che Guevara, the thousands killed resisting oppression from Indochina to Latin America, the thousands more in jail—the unfinished litany of witnesses? Just how far would we like to go into the world of mass victims and silently responsible executioners (with obscurely familiar faces)? How far into the lives of men and women caged in slums and tunneled under jungles who demand release from that world and whose needs, when seen and felt, move us to either impotent shame or the decision to resist inhumanity? Just how far would we like to go

with our lives into the suffering truth which commits
people to liberation through resistance?

Not too far but just far enough so's we can say that
we've been there.

The truth of the cross and the empty tomb, the truth
of crucifixion-resurrection, is not a speculative or tenta-
tive truth. Not too far but just far enough so's we can
say that we've been there—is nowhere for liberation. We
go in or we stay out. Zen doesn't open to the curious.
Jesus didn't try out the cross to see if his faith would
work. The only feasible experiment with the truth of
liberation is Gandhi's experiment in truth, the kind of
inquiry into the power and demands of truth which
Gandhi undertook each day of his life with as much care
as any lab technician ever took in treating explosive chem-
icals. Gandhi's seriousness with truth was a simple reflection of his uncompromising willingness to act on the truth
with his whole life once he discovered its way. The
truth of liberation taken seriously is a way of life and
of suffering resistance to the powers, a way of freedom
with an admission price—my whole life in the service
of truth. The martyred apostles of liberation, observing
the homage we pay them, ask with their eyes wide as
tigers, "And just how far would you like to go in?"

Americans whose faith in social change passed through
the commitments and assassinations of the '6os are afraid
that they have already gone too far in, and many have
retreated. They have already seen and experienced too
much of the world's truth, while a succession of dead
leaders and widening slums and wars have ended an
earlier vision. Jack Newfield, a writer who began by
chronicling the birth and growth of the New Left which

he participated in,[1] concludes a later memoir of Robert Kennedy in a way characteristic of the change in attitude, with a generation's sense of extinguished vision:

> Now I realized what makes our generation unique, what defines us apart from those who came before the hopeful winter of 1961, and those who came after the murderous spring of 1968. We are the first generation that learned from experience, in our innocent twenties, that things were not really getting better, that we shall *not* overcome. We felt, by the time we reached thirty, that we had already glimpsed the most compassionate leaders our nation could produce, and they had all been assassinated. And from this time forward, things would get worse: our best political leaders were part of memory now, not hope.
>
> The stone was at the bottom of the hill and we were alone.[2]

This resting place of Camus' rock of Sisyphus, which rolled back hopelessly on a generation in 1968, had already been seen in 1965 by Dylan in his great song "Like a Rolling Stone":

> You've gone to the finest school all right, Miss Lonely,
> But you know you only used to get juiced in it.
> And nobody's ever taught you
> How to live on the street
> And now you're gonna have to get used to it . . .
>
> How does it feel, How does it feel,
> To be without a home,
> Like a complete unknown. Like a rolling stone?[3]

---

[1] Jack Newfield, *A Prophetic Minority* (Signet: 1967).

[2] Jack Newfield, *Robert Kennedy: A Memoir* (Bantam Books: 1970), p. 348.

[3] "Like a Rolling Stone" (Bob Dylan) © 1965 by M. Witmark & Sons. Used by Permission of Warner Bros. Music. All Rights Reserved.

Although Dylan was singing about more than the New Left, Miss Lonely out on the street with no direction home embodied the stripping of illusions which the believers in non-violence and a democratic society were forced to suffer relentlessly for the rest of the decade, from the hopes of Montgomery and Port Huron to the despair of Memphis and Chicago. After Memphis, Los Angeles, Chicago, Cambodia, Laos . . . , just how far can we go now into the reality of liberation?

But left alone at the bottom of the hill, or out on the street as Miss Lonely, stripped of the hope to liberate a dying society through direct action, we are freer now to think through the nature of liberation itself, and to enter into a dimension of liberation which includes yet goes deeper than the struggle for civil rights, the end of the war, and participatory democracy. Alone at the bottom of the hill, we can begin to understand our own evasions of truth. For in our politically saturated time an overt commitment to resist the powers of oppression may serve in its own way as an avoidance of the ultimate demands of truth. We may discover that simply to have resisted the powers was not to have gone very far into liberation after all—or to have gone only half the way to truth, a truth which is undivided, so that half the way to truth is nowhere in reality. Just far enough so's we can say that we've been there, "Yes, we resisted, now we're somewhere else," nowhere in either case. Liberation is much more than resistance, and to have gone no deeper than resistance is to have missed the truth of liberation and of resistance itself.

The deeper half of liberation is contemplation, and contemplation begins alone at the bottom of the hill, or out on the street as Miss Lonely. To contemplate is to look intently at reality, and to begin to see it as it is. Contemplation begins with a sharp perception of our rock-bottom poverty and powerlessness—not so much in the sense of leaders assassinated and campaigns destroyed, the preliminaries to a deeper onslaught, as in the sense of an individual self exposed finally without props and pretensions. As what? As nothing, as emptiness, as a vacant stretch ahead with no direction home. When society has replied to the advocates of change by blasting concrete hopes held so deeply that they served as the political and social props of a generation's existence, people are left without bearings, occupying blank spaces. But the very blankness and silence contains a new beginning and a deeper possibility. Contemplation as a bedrock base for liberation can begin to be known for the first time only when each of us is left alone to face himself.

Alfred Delp, a Jesuit priest writing from a prison cell in Nazi Germany while awaiting his execution, described the supreme importance to man of this contemplative encounter in the wilderness:

> Great issues affecting mankind always have to be decided in the wilderness, in uninterrupted isolation and unbroken silence. They hold a meaning and a blessing these great, silent, empty spaces that bring a man face to face with reality . . .
> The wilderness has a necessary function in life. "Abandonment" one of my friends called it and the word is very apt. Abandonment to wind and weather and day and night and all the intervening hours. And abandonment to the silence of God, the greatest abandonment of all. The virtue that thrives most on it—patience—is

the most necessary of all virtues that spring from the heart—and the Spirit.[4]

Contemplation begins in the wilderness because man must be left alone to recognize how in fact he is always alone. The initial shock of the wilderness is cold but necessary: How does it feel? How does it feel? To be without a home. Like a complete unknown. Like a rolling stone. The chilling poverty of Miss Lonely out on the street remains the fundamental condition of us all, a condition simply made more obvious in a time of crisis.

The Newfield memoir of Robert Kennedy makes clear that the Kennedy who began to identify with and speak out for the disinherited of America was born only after the shock and crisis of his brother's assassination. He grew to new character during the period of withdrawal and contemplation which was an existential night. In a profoundly personal sense, there was no Robert Kennedy until after the assassination had taken the brother in whom he had submerged his life, thus throwing him back on his own existence and resources—first perceived as emptiness. The contemplative way of liberation begins with the shock of recognizing the bedrock poverty of one's self.

Resistance and contemplation combine to seek the liberation of man from a twofold poverty: the poverty of the world which subjects living children to rats and starvation, and the root poverty of man's own self which is alone and impotent to overcome the world.

The full truth of liberation is like the *Tao*, or the Way, realized through a *yin-yang* movement in all things. In Taoist mysticism, yin and yang are complementary as-

[4] Alfred Delp, S.J., *The Prison Meditations of Father Alfred Delp* (Herder and Herder: 1963), pp. 95, 97.

pects of a single Reality, seen in the polarities of active-passive, bright-dark, firm-yielding, etc. The union of yin-yang differences yields the wholeness through which the Tao is known. The meaning of yin-yang, like its symbol◐, cannot be grasped unless it is perceived in its entirety. Yin and yang are meaningless in themselves; they are necessary to each other.

If resistance is the yang of the Way of Liberation, then contemplation is its yin. The two are one, indivisible reality, and it is through them as one that the Way of Liberation is known. If we wish to pass into the living truth of Jesus and Gandhi, we must affirm, as they did, the Way of Liberation as neither the yang of resistance nor the yin of contemplation but rather as the one, indivisible Way, standing both within and transcendent to the yin-yang of resistance and contemplation.

As resistance seeks to liberate men and women from the pain of social injustice, contemplation seeks to liberate us from the pain of a yet deeper alienation, an impoverished and autonomous self. Man if liberated from his false self is united with the One, and personal separation and pain are overcome in the harmony of pure Being. Liberation in its contemplative form predates the liberation fronts of today's global revolution. The contemplative basis for liberation was laid in the East, in a way of wisdom initiated in India more than a thousand years before Christ: the way of *moksha* or liberation of man from the law of *karma*. Besides the classic Hindu formulation, the way took further form in the enlightenment of Siddhartha Gautama, the historic Buddha; in the mysticism of Taoism, the original Chinese way of liberation; and in the amalgam of Taoism and Indian Mahayana Buddhism which occurred in China and produced Zen. Contemplation is familiar to Western Christians in the monastic traditions which trace their origins to the early Desert Fathers, but it is in the Eastern religions that contemplation has played its most central role of liberation. It is to the East, and to Zen in particular, that Western contemplatives today look increasingly for guidance.

The significance of contemplation in its specific—and in today's world, indispensable—relation to resistance, as the yin-yang of a personally and socially embrasive Way of Liberation, can be drawn from some of the final words of a great Western monk who died on his journey to the East, Thomas Merton. A few hours before his accidental death by electrocution on December 10, 1968, at a monastery in Bangkok, Merton gave a talk on "Marxist Theory and Monastic Theoria." The background for the talk was the work of Herbert Marcuse: "And I would add quite bluntly and brutally that I regard him as a kind of monastic thinker, so that if you want to be completely irresponsible you could say that this is a conference on the monastic implications of Marcuse at the present time."[5]

In the talk, Merton gives two concrete illustrations which speak simply and profoundly, first, of the existential situation we have already glimpsed through a political impasse, and secondly, of the contemplative response to that situation.

[5] I have been able to compare two separate transcripts of Merton's last talk. In the three excerpts quoted here, the only more than incidental difference between transcripts comes in Merton's identification of the source of the saying, "Where do you go from the top of a thirty-foot pole?", which reads in one "The German people have a saying . . ." and in the other, which I have quoted, "The Zen people . . ." I am grateful to Bob Aitken for pointing out that the reference is probably to "Sekiso's Hundred-Foot Pole." See R. H. Blyth, *Mumonkan; Zen and Zen Classics,* Vol. IV (Hokuseido Press, Tokyo: 1966), pp. 295–300.

After dwelling on Marcuse's theory that all highly organized technological societies end up by being equally totalitarian in one way or another, Merton brings the significance of this home by telling the conference of monks the story of a Tibetan lama. This friend of Merton's had to leave Tibet or be killed when the Chinese Communists took over all the Tibetan monasteries. The lama was isolated in the mountains, living in a peasant's house and wondering what to do next. He sent a message to a nearby abbot friend of his, saying "What do we do?" The abbot sent back a strange message which Merton found extremely significant. The abbot said, "From now on, brother, everybody stands on his own feet."

Merton comments on this message:

> To my mind that is an extremely important monastic statement. If you forget everything else that has been said, I would suggest that you remember this for the future: "From now on, everybody stands on his own feet." This, I think, is what Buddhism is about, it is what Christianity is about, what monasticism is about, if you understand it in terms of grace. That is to say (it is not a Pelagian statement by any means), that we can no longer rely on being supported by structures which may be destroyed at any moment by a political power, or political force. You cannot rely on structures. The time for relying on structures has disappeared. They are good, and they should help us, and we should do the best we can with them. But they may be taken away, and if everything is taken away, what do you do next?

> The Zen people have a saying which has nothing directly to do with this, but it is analogous in a certain sense: "Where do you go from the top of a thirty-foot pole?" Well, in a certain way, the answer has something in common: "Where do you go from the top of a thirty-foot pole?" Which is where we all now sit, and I think it is

useful in this conference to take account of the fact that that is where we are.

From now on, brother, everybody stands on his own feet. The time for relying on structures has disappeared. How does it feel? To be on your own. With no direction home. The stone is at the bottom of the hill and we are alone. If everything is taken away, what do you do next? Where do you go from the top of a thirty-foot pole? For that is where we all are now, brothers and sisters.

Merton's second illustration, and a moving one to conclude a talk and his life, is a depiction of one of the traditional representations of the Buddha. The Buddha is seated in the lotus posture; in one hand he holds a begging bowl, and with the other he is pointing to the earth. The gesture of pointing to the earth has been made in response to an accusation by Mara, the tempter who represents all illusion. Mara had come to Buddha, who had attained Enlightenment, and said, "You have no business sitting on that little square of earth where you are sitting because it belongs to me." The Buddha pointed to the earth, and called it to witness that it did not belong to Mara, because he had just attained enlightenment on it.

Merton comments:

This is a very excellent statement, I think, about the relation of the monk to the world. The monk belongs to the world, but the world belongs to him insofar as he has dedicated himself totally to liberation from it, in order to liberate it. You can't just immerse yourself in the world, and get carried away with it. That is no salvation. If you want to pull a drowning man out of the water, you have to have some support yourself.

Supposing somebody is drowning, and you are standing on a rock, you can do it. Or supposing you can support yourself by swimming, you can do it. There is nothing to be gained by simply jumping in the water and drowning with him.

There is no sensitive conscience which can confront the global organization of power today, and its apparently uncontrollable technology, without seeing that the people are indeed drowning. They are drowning everywhere, and they are going down fast. If the horsemen of the Apocalypse continue to gallop faster, there will soon be no stopping their sweep across the entire world, beating into dust and bones every illusion which mankind has managed to sustain to this point in history. The words of another Dylan song catch the mood of that impending scene:

> All along the watchtower
> Princes kept the view
> While all the women came and went
> Barefoot servants too.
> Outside in the distance
> A wildcat did growl.
> Two riders were approaching.
> The wind began to howl.[6]

The people are drowning, or more exactly, they are being drowned by a system which submerges humanity beneath enormous power apparently controlled by a few but perhaps by no one. For the sake of everyone's humanity, a response is necessary. But to respond to the people and to resist the power of that system without a rock to stand on is simply to jump in the water and drown with the people. Merton suggests that the contemplative

[6] "All Along the Watchtower," © Dwarf Music, 1968.

has a rock to stand on—he has dedicated himself totally to liberation from the world in order to liberate it—but from where most of us stand, the rock of contemplative liberation, the square of earth on which the Buddha sits, remains indistinct both in itself and in relation to the needs of the people.

Archimedes once said that he could move the world if he could be given a place outside the world to stand. And Merton himself has said elsewhere where we might begin to look to find this place outside the world, this rock on which to stand. He refers to the Buddhist rejection of a naïve and activistic doctrine of revolution by force, and points out further how a particular Buddhist writer questions rather astutely

> the Western acceptance of a "will to transform others" in terms of one's own prophetic insight accepted as a norm of pure justice. Is there not an "optical illusion" in an eschatological spirit which, however much it may appeal to *agape,* seeks only to transform persons and social structures *from the outside?* Here we arrive at a basic principle, one might almost say an ontology of nonviolence, which requires further investigation.[7] (emphasis in original)

Hints such as this, found in the concluding words of one of Thomas Merton's last books, *Mystics and Zen Masters,* lead one to the examination of roots: the roots of the Gospel, of Zen, of Reality.

A key term in the Gospel—one on which Jesus' entire statement pivots—is *metanoia.* *Metanoia* is the unavoidable imperative which we all seek to avoid, a demand placed upon us by existence itself. A Greek word mean-

---

[7] Thomas Merton, *Mystics and Zen Masters* (Delta Book: 1967), pp. 287–88.

ing literally "change of mind," *metanoia* in its Gospel sense cuts like a karate chop through our well-worn schemes and justifications: We thought we knew who we were and where we were going. We had a lot invested in that knowing of ours. But it all managed to avoid the real issues. That's what *metanoia*'s all about: down with our elaborate justifications![8]

Metanoia is the absolute demand made on every man that he turn away from his self and that he turn toward the One who can finally become present only through the wrenching emptiness of man's self-renunciation. The way Jesus put it was, "The time has come, and the kingdom of God is close at hand. *Repent*, and believe the Good News" (Mark 1:15). And more explicitly: "If anyone wants to be a follower of mine, let him renounce himself and take up his cross and follow me. For anyone who wants to save his life will lose it; but anyone who loses his life for my sake, and for the sake of the gospel, will save it" (Mark 8:34-35).

Metanoia is the demand for that wrench away from my household idols to confront the living God. If I dared to carry it through, it would result in my becoming a new man, someone whom I do not know and whom I fear to know. I will do anything I can to avoid recognizing the imperative of metanoia because my self is terrified by the prospect it opens up of a future in which the self has been renounced and its demands laid to rest. For what, after all, can there be left for me without *me*? Nothing; yet it is precisely there, in nothingness, that metanoia claims to expose the rock on which to stand, the Buddha's square of earth. For it is just

[8] Thanks to Dave Burrell for the exposition of metanoia in this paragraph.

there, at the point where one has renounced every scheme
of his, that Jesus presumes to lay on man the full
burden of existence. It is only then, after letting go
of a grasping self, that a man is prepared to join Jesus
in resisting the powers—to "take up his cross and follow
me"; to trial, imprisonment, death; to whatever these
may mean in the living reality of one's own resistance.

The rock which appears in the metanoia of Jesus is
the second half of his statement: "Repent, and *believe
the Good News.*" Renunciation empties one out for the
sake of faith. Metanoia leads to that total inner transformation which Jesus calls faith. If Jesus is to be taken
seriously, faith is the rock to stand upon: "Have faith
in God. I tell you solemnly, if anyone says to this mountain, 'Get up and throw yourself into the sea,' with no
hesitation in his heart but believing that what he says
will happen, it will be done for him" (Mark 11:22-23).
In the face of centuries of theology, we might be per-
mitted one observation about the rock that is faith: if
it exists, few people have stood upon it. Or again:
if many have stood upon it, few have realized what
Archimedes hypothesized, that they might then have
been in a position to move the world.

The Zen equivalent of metanoia is *satori*. *Satori*, or
"awakening," is the acquiring of an absolutely new point
of view toward life and the world, or an intuitive looking
into the nature or suchness of things, as opposed to a
verbal or analytic understanding of them. D. T. Suzuki,
the greatest expositor of Zen to the West, has said:
"Whatever can be named leads to dualism, and Buddhism is not dualistic. To take hold of this non-duality
of truth is the aim of Zen."[9] Satori demands that one

[9] D. T. Suzuki, *Essays in Zen Buddhism* (*First Series*) (Grove Press:
1961), p. 212.

surrender his separate ego, and promises beyond all dualisms a liberating flash of the profound unity of existence. Satori is the outcome of an inward struggle to be freed from an autonomous ideal of the self and from all the frustrated cravings of a self-defined world. Merton called satori "the explosive rediscovery of the hidden and lost reality within us,"[10] "the recovery of Paradise."[11] Suzuki said its discovery came through the realization of Emptiness, "seeing into the nonexistence of a thingish ego-substance"[12] and being poor in spirit. To be absolutely nothing is to be everything, or in the double equation of Suzuki, zero=infinity and infinity=zero. Zero is no self, no ego. Out of this zero the infinite is realized, and the state of Paradise is recovered in an innocence of one-thought-viewing. But the way back to Paradise is barred by an angel with a flaming sword turning every way, so that all who wish to return must be tested by the fire. Like metanoia, the fulfillment of Zen in the enlightenment of satori stands at the end of a self-renunciation: "Emptiness, poverty, death or dissolution—they are all realized when one goes through the experiences of 'breaking through' . . ."[13] To be absolutely naked of all things, and even of the experience of satori itself, is the goal of Zen training.

Suzuki and Merton agree that Zen is not concerned with theology but only with life itself. Creation, not creator, is the stuff of Zen. "To see into the work of creation and not interview the creator himself"[14] is the aim of

[10] *Mystics and Zen Masters,* p. 50.

[11] Thomas Merton, *Zen and the Birds of Appetite* (New Directions: 1968), p. 116.

[12] Suzuki in his dialogue with Merton in *Zen and the Birds of Appetite,* p. 109.

[13] Suzuki in *Zen and the Birds of Appetite,* p. 114.

[14] *Essays in Zen Buddhism (First Series),* p. 263.

Zen (Suzuki). By liberating man from a restrictive ego, the Zen discipline allows him to open his eyes and see. What he sees is a void which is infinite. What he sees is the suchness of things. What he sees is indescribably one. The perception of Zen is an instantaneous, living insight into being, so that we look at things as they are and so that we live now, on the ground where we are standing.

We don't know what it is that Jesus saw, but the Gospel suggests a Zen-like perception. At the same time Suzuki and Merton agree that Jesus added a new dimension—that of faith—to the ontological contemplation of reality which is Zen. Jesus' "Zen" expression of this new dimension of faith occurs in the Sermon on the Mount:

> Look at the birds in the sky. They do not sow or reap or gather into barns; yet your heavenly Father feeds them . . . And why worry about clothing? Think of the flowers growing in the fields; they never have to work or spin; yet I assure you that not even Solomon in all his regalia was robed like one of these . . . So do not worry; do not say, "What are we to eat? What are we to drink? How are we to be clothed?" It is the pagans who set their hearts on all these things. Your heavenly Father knows you need them all. Set your hearts on his kingdom first, and on his righteousness, and all these other things will be given you as well. (Matt. 6:26, 28-29, 31-33)

Suzuki finds this passage embodies "the spirit of Zen"[15] because of Jesus' "ordinary mindedness" toward the birds and the flowers and his counsel of no thought for food, drink, or the morrow. But it articulates as well the spirit of the Father and his kingdom. Life is to be seen, experienced as it is, yet the kingdom remains to be built. The union of Zen and a living, working faith in the Father's kingdom is testimony both that the kingdom

15 *Ibid.*, p. 302.

is not ideological and that life itself is not indifferent to a loving justice as the culmination of history. The kingdom gathers up the multiple tensions ingredient in life itself as Jesus prays: "Thy will be done on earth as it is in heaven."

Satori and metanoia reveal an imperative of existence itself, and spell out the demand behind the demands which reduce a man to nothingness: How does it feel to be on your own, with no direction home, a complete unknown? Because that's the way it *is*, Miss Lonely, the way reality seeks to come home to your still unbelieving, unself-denying self. Reality comes home in desolation. The self is alone and exposed but it holds on desperately in the face of judgment: How does it feel? How does it feel? Perhaps the self begins, ever so slightly, to turn. The poet Dylan follows the shock and judgment of reality in "Like a Rolling Stone" with a more gentle invitation in "Queen Jane Approximately":

> Now when all the clowns that you have commissioned
> Have died in battle or in vain
> And you're sick of all this repetition
> Won't you come see me, Queen Jane
> Won't you come see me, Queen Jane[16]

As the self finally shows signs of loosening its grip, reality's judgment becomes an invitation to faith and the kingdom: Won't you come see me, Queen Jane?[17]

[16] "Queen Jane Approximately" (Bob Dylan) © 1965 by M. Witmark & Sons. Used by Permission of Warner Bros. Music. All Rights Reserved.

[17] Dylan's later songs, beginning with the album *Blond on Blond,* can be understood best as a deepening statement of the kingdom. See the beautiful article by Steven Goldberg, "Bob Dylan and the Poetry of Salvation" (*Saturday Review:* May 30, 1970), which covers the period up to *Nashville Skyline.* In *New Morning,* the kingdom is described as both Zen ("New Morning") and the Gospel ("Father of Night").

Mike McKale says that it's the other way around, "New Morning" is the Gospel and "Father of Night" is Zen, and I believe he's right, too, depending on which way one leans in listening to each song: "New

But to begin to envision the way of the kingdom, the summit of liberation, it is helpful to consider again the yin-yang relation of resistance and contemplation, and to do this through a reflection on the yin-yang doctrine as it is found in its classic Chinese source, the *I Ching* or *Book of Changes.*

As we saw, the solitude which bears down everywhere on human existence began to be experienced as a crushing reality by Americans when their faith in social change was extinguished by the murderous events and climate of the late '60s. A freshly radical faith in social change was crushed under the hammerblows of corporate America. But some discovered they too had a hammer, one they could use to forge a yet more solid base for liberation, "a rock outside the world to stand upon." So the destruction of a naïve and illusory faith, the shock of a reality resistant to my collective self and *its* idea of change, forced us to search for a more deeply liberating change, that change of mind and heart which is metanoia, the change to a totally new point of view which is satori. Liberation, the common factor in resistance and contemplation, is thus, on a still simpler level of understanding, the reality of change—the change profoundly necessary to a world and a self which mirror each other in their frustrated yearnings for freedom.

The concept of change found in the *I Ching,* or *Book*

Morning" is the good news of a new world. But it's also the Zen of that world, "Can't you hear . . . ?, Can't you feel . . . ?" "Father of Night" is darkness, birds flying, and mountains so high. But it's also the creator teaching, building, and shaping, "who dwells in our hearts and our memories." Maybe the point, yin-yang again, is that the faith of the Gospel enables one to see the world of creation, as the blind discovered when they were given sight by Jesus, and that one must first see that world in order to believe the Gospel: "Look at the birds in the sky. They do not sow or reap or gather into barns; yet your heavenly Father . . ."

of Change, is that of the Tao. The Tao, or "Way," is the active power in the universe as a whole and in each of its parts, the way on which we must all walk. The Tao is the way, it is the walker, it is the walking itself on that way. "The Tao stands all by itself, all alone, and yet walks about everywhere."[18] The Tao is everywhere and nowhere. It is realized only in the walking, so it cannot be measured or mapped out in advance.

The Tao is the constant in change. Change is the movement we experience in our lives, the stream in which we find ourselves and in which we feel we are losing ourselves—unless we can perceive something constant or secure in the movement of change. The Tao is the great principle, the constant way discoverable in change. It can be understood through the dynamic polar tension which runs through reality and which is expressed in *The Book of Change* by a succession of paired concepts: creative and receptive, active and acted upon, firm and yielding, each of these expressing a face of the co-ordinate concepts of yin and yang.

Yin and yang are the forces of change which make up existence, are mutually dependent, and give expression to the Way. They are dynamic forces. As Hellmut Wilhelm, one of the foremost scholars on the *I Ching,* has put it:

> It is impossible to overemphasize the dynamism of this process. Polarity here does not mean rigidity, nor a pole around which the cyclic movement turns, but a "magnetic field" which determines the change, indeed evokes it.[19]

[18] D. T. Suzuki, Introduction to *The Texts of Taoism,* translated by James Legge (The Julian Press: 1959), p. 14.
[19] Hellmut Wilhelm, *Change: Eight Lectures on the I Ching* (Harper Torchbooks: 1964), p. 27.

As for the locus of yin-yang change, it is everywhere, but especially in man:

> From this comprehensiveness of tao, embracing both macrocosm and microcosm, the Book of Changes derives the idea that man is in the center of events; the individual who is conscious of responsibility is on a par with the cosmic forces of heaven and earth . . . Since every seed attains development in change, it must also be possible to introduce into its flow a seed planted by man. And since knowledge of the laws of change teaches the right way of placing such a seed, a highly effective influence becomes possible.[20]

In short, what is necessary for a man to bring about change in his own time is that he rediscover in himself the yin-yang dynamism of change, which knowledge if disciplined and directed will permit him to plant a revolutionary seed of his own in the flow of change. The seed will come from and will be himself. And as his action becomes a more single-minded expression of the yin and yang of his own self-acceptance and self-renunciation, *he* will disappear and the seed will bear fruit. The yin-yang dynamism is discoverable now as contemplation and resistance.

The basis for identifying yin with contemplation and yang with resistance is, first of all, the most ancient understanding of the doctrine itself. The earliest written character used by the Chinese for yin was the character for "cloud," and thus meant "the overcast," "the dark." Implicit in the early image for yin is the idea of life-giving water as a dispenser of nourishment. The earliest character for yang, on the other hand, shows a pennant waving in the sun, and thus meant "something gleaming

[20] *Ibid.*, p. 22.

in the light," "the bright." Implicit in the yang picture is the power of command which raises the banner. In a later development, the classifier signifying "mountain slope" was added to both yin and yang, so that yin came to mean "the dark-shadowed side of the slope," and yang the bright, sunlit side.[21]

Yin: receptive, yielding, life-giving water, the cloud, the dark slope of the mountain—contemplation. Yang: active, firm, the power of command, the banner waving in the sun, the bright side of the mountain—resistance. According to one of the old masters of Sung philosophy, "Now yin, now yang, that is tao."[22] Contemplation, resistance are the way of liberation.

In this essay toward an understanding of liberation, we began with a commitment of resistance, which led to the deeper need for contemplation. Having arrived at the base of liberation in yin-yang, contemplation and resistance, let us explore now first the dark-shadowed, then the sunlit slope of the mountain, climbing as we explore, in the hope of arriving finally at the summit of liberation, that kingdom which gives a view of both its sides and assumes a living experience of their terrain.

The dark-shadowed side of the mountain: I am alone on it. I see no one, hear nothing but the sound of the wind in the trees, and its howl across the slope up ahead where the trees thin into bare ground. It is cold, my clothes are light, and the wind hits my back and pushes me into further movement up the slope. The power of the wind makes me struggle to keep my feet. As the trees

[21] *Ibid.*, p. 30. See also Richard Wilhelm, Introduction to the *I Ching* or *Book of Change,* translated by Richard Wilhelm and Cary F. Baynes (Bollingen Series XIX, Princeton University Press: 1967), p. lvi.

[22] Chou Tun-i in his treatise called the *I-t'ung shu,* the Book for the Explaining of the *I Ching.* Quoted by Hellmut Wilhelm in *Change,* p. 89.

fall behind, the path I am following becomes indistinct, illegible. It, too, disappears. There is no way ahead, only the mountain slope, the cold, the wind, and a summit which is unattainable because I cannot see how to attain it. The wind keeps pushing me, knocking me off balance, but there is no way I can see to keep going, just the dark mountain which reaches up, becomes a sheer wall of rock, and there is nothing I can do to reach the top. I am alone, freezing against the rock wall in the dark, no longer climbing, just fighting to stand against the wind, when suddenly I let the full force of the wind push me out into dark space: the summit and life-giving water. I am not there but I know the way.

The sunlit side of the mountain: Here it is crowded, men shouldering their way along, brightened by the sun, but most of them coming down the slope and carrying unseen knives. Their children are at the bottom. The men do not realize they are carrying knives, and they do not realize their children are at the bottom. Least of all do they see the outcome of their descent. They are men of good will traveling fast. We are only a few but we have realized the presence of our knives and have turned them inward so as to climb the mountain and resist the downward rush. We are only a few, and what can a few do to stop so many trampling feet? But we get together, raise our cries and our banner to the crowd, and stand to meet them. The crowd, in a hurry, blinded by the sun, comes down on us, pushes, hits out. As we stand against the blows, we see the beauty of the faces one by one and their children in their faces: the summit, banner waving in the sun, the human family gathered beneath it. We are not there but we know the way.

The yin of contemplation is an encounter on the dark

side of the mountain, in the soul. Contemplation, the struggle to experience reality as it is, in the life-giving water of the One, is the acceptance of the upward wind of the Spirit and the disciplined loss of my self-control. I struggle for the power of the powerless, where I would lose my self, where only the Spirit moves and zero= infinity. The Spirit is received through a painful resistance to, and renunciation of, the claims of the self on the climb into greater darkness. Contemplation receives by resisting. At its center contemplation is receptivity to the wind of the Spirit, but it is conditioned by my active resistance to the fears and claims of the self: claims of comfort, security, self-control.

The yang of resistance, on the bright slope, is the struggle to stand against a murderous collective self and to express communally the living unity of all men in the One. Resistance is active opposition to the death forces discernible in every modern state. The confrontation of resistance therefore takes place on the bright side of the mountain, in the sunlight of public or collective consciousness, where men struggle with the powers of war, racism, exploitation. But resistance cannot stand its ground alone. Against the collective forces of death, it holds only that ground—the Buddha's square of earth— which has been secured by contemplation. Resistance is known by its public stand, but it is a stand defined by personal receptivity to a vision of inner power, whereby a man discovers in his inmost being that undivided humanity which his banner proclaims.

The contemplative yin and resistant yang are co-ordinate powers of change which reinforce each other on a single way of liberation: liberation from a divided and divisive self in both its individual and collective forms;

liberation into the One, where person, community, reality realize their ultimate identity. Yin becomes yang, contemplation passes into resistance, for the struggle on the dark side has freed me to recognize in the sunlight the murderousness of the collective self as my own self written large. And a life sinking roots in the living water has strengthened me to see and live for the One in all men.

Yang without yin is no liberation, no change: To resist without seeking to shed the skin of the individual self is not to resist at all. It is simply to confront the power of the world with a smaller, antagonistic version of itself. To resist with the self is to surrender to its embodiment in the world.

Yin without yang is no liberation, no change: To contemplate without seeking to shed the collective self of totalitarian institutions is not to contemplate at all. It is simply to build the fall-out shelter of an esthetic spirituality and to seek refuge in ruins. To contemplate being without resisting the destruction of the living is to contemplate the self.

Now yin, now yang, is the way: To resist as the new man, and to contemplate being under the banner of resistance, is to stand solidly on that rock outside the world, the rock of faith, and to move the mountain of injustice. Yin-yang ushers in the kingdom.

Before the encounters on the sunlit side—before he was tortured and executed for resistance, before he confronted the power of the Sanhedrin, before he knocked over the tables of the money changers in the temple, before he flayed publicly the righteousness of the Pharisees, before he called men to pick up their own crosses and come along—before all this, Jesus went into the desert for a long time. The Gospels say he was led there by the Spirit. What he saw in the desert we do not know, but it is said that the tempter came to him with three ways to seize power. From the story of Jesus' encounter with Satan, after a forty-day fast in the wilderness, we learn that contemplation is a solitary struggle with the temptation of power, and a renunciation of it for the sake of resistance and liberation into the kingdom.

Jesus' first temptation to seize power was that of economic power: "If you are the Son of God, tell these stones to turn into loaves." A perceptive commentator has said of this first temptation:

> . . . surely it was not his own hunger alone that was in Jesus' thoughts in these desert days. There was the hunger of the great multitudes of the world's poor . . . it was a question of the regular method to be adopted for his whole public career . . . First the earthly paradise, then the heavenly paradise—was that not the right order?[23]

The Gospel narratives tell us that Jesus did in fact respond later to the hunger of the multitude following him. But he did so only occasionally, in response to a particular need, not as a primary statement of the Gospel. Jesus' method in igniting men's faith followed instead the sense of his response to Satan: "Man does not live on bread alone but on every word that comes from the mouth of God." Every word from the mouth of God— that man might listen to that word in himself and fill his life with it—was the primary factor for Jesus, not the satisfaction of man's physical hunger, as it would have

[23] James Stuart Stewart, *The Life and Teaching of Jesus Christ.*

been had he consulted an economic planner for the kingdom.

There is no question but that Jesus' position here is a
scandalous one for the modern consciousness. There are
few of us who are not thoroughgoing Marxists on this
point. We believe in the priority of physical food over
the truth. And our understanding of the methodology of
social change is derived from that priority: In order to
change conditions of intolerable injustice, let us direct
our primary efforts toward changing the economic sub-
structure. But Jesus rejected this understanding of
change: Man does not live on bread alone. Therefore
Jesus' response to the hunger of the masses is not that of
turning stones into bread. He emphasizes a different
kind of bread, a different kind of change, while he shares
personally the most basic needs of the people, intensely
so at the end of a forty-day fast.

The basis of the economic temptation, then as now, is
our own power under the guise of a politically realistic
humanism: *We* must somehow turn stones into bread
(capitalism and class conflict into shared resources) or
the people will perish. The point of Jesus' response to
Satan is that man, the people, will live irrespective of
your and my efforts to transform stones. The people's
need for liberation goes deeper than our particular techniques for saving them, and in fact the bread in every
sense will come through that deeper kind of liberation,
not by some political or technological savior's giving it to
them.

The point is made by Paulo Freire in his *Pedagogy of
the Oppressed*, where he warns of the revolutionary
leader's temptation to take advantage of the emotional

dependence of the oppressed, especially by accentuating their need for bread when their liberation involves a more radical struggle:

> The oppressed, who have been shaped by the death-affirming climate of oppression, must find through their struggle the way to life-affirming humanization, which does not lie *simply* in having more to eat (although it does involve having more to eat and cannot fail to include this aspect). The oppressed have been destroyed precisely because their situation has reduced them to things. In order to regain their humanity they must cease to be things and fight as men. This is a radical requirement. They cannot enter the struggle as objects in order *later* to become men.[24] (emphasis in original)

The temptation is a subtle one. The oppressed need bread desperately. And it is true, as Gandhi said, that God comes to starving men in the form of bread. Nevertheless man does not live on bread alone, and the people do not depend on the revolutionary leader's transformation of stones into bread. Liberation is deeper, more personal, and more radical than that, and the contemplative struggle in the desert reveals that the way of liberation is not open to him who aspires to his own power through the people's need for bread.

Jesus' second temptation (according to the order of Matthew's account) was that of spiritual power:

> The devil then took him to the holy city and made him stand on the parapet of the Temple. "If you are the Son of God," he said "throw yourself down; for scripture says: 'He will put you in his angels' charge, and they will support you on their hands in case you hurt your

[24] Paulo Freire, *Pedagogy of the Oppressed* (Herder and Herder: 1970), p. 55.

foot against a stone.'" Jesus said to him, "Scripture also says: 'You must not put the Lord your God to the test.'" (Matt. 4:5–7)

A man utterly alone in the desert, eating nothing, seeking the reality of truth and his life's mission, must begin to experience his powerlessness, begin to drop toward zero. But the drop to zero is infinite, and somewhere in the despair of the self's fall a vision intervenes: On the parapet of the Temple—*this* is the right setting, *here* the invitation to a spiritual commitment of sonship. Yes, throw yourself down, not alone in a wasteland but here, as an effective demonstration of mission, as a spiritually relevant act whereby men may see God's power, see it bear one up out of the depths. Drop toward zero, but do so somewhere in the arena of power so that the drop itself and the infinity which is bound to meet you before zero might serve as an effective witness for others.

One biblical scholar has suggested that what Jesus envisioned in the temptation may have been a comforting scenario of the death penalty he feared on the horizon: not by crucifixion but by being thrown down from a tower in the temple wall into the Kidron Valley, followed by stoning if necessary to bring death, the prescribed penalty for blasphemy.[25] The hope of divine intervention would then have been the same temptation that Jesus suffered through in Gethsemane in his prayer to the Father, and again at Golgotha in the form of the spectators' taunts that he demonstrate God's power by coming down from the cross. But neither an avoidance of the end nor a substitution of spiritual relevance for complete emptiness

[25] Niels Hyldahl, *Studia Theologica* XV (1961), 113 ff. John Howard Yoder provided the Hyldahl and Stewart references in his draft, "The Possibility of a Messianic Ethic" (April 1968).

was possible. The drop into zero had to be accomplished
in resistance on the cross just as it was in contemplation
in the desert, in stark emptiness, for infinity to be realized. Jesus' rejection of the second temptation signifies
that in the desert, on the dark side of the mountain, there
is no spiritual power—only the Spirit itself leading one
into a more and more desolate wasteland, the power of
the powerless.

The third temptation: from a mountain, a vision of all
the kingdoms of the world and their glory. Naked political power. But the temptation went much deeper than
sheer power—it was power with a redeeming purpose:
power for the liberation of Jesus' people.

We often forget the facts of the case: (1) The Jewish
people were an occupied nation, under the garrison of
imperial Rome. (2) Jesus lived intensely in the context
of his people's burning passion for freedom from Rome.
At least one of the chosen Twelve, Simon the Zealot, and
perhaps as many as half of them, were Zealot revolutionaries, who expected Jesus to lead them in an armed
revolution and were bitterly disappointed when he did
not. (3) Jesus was crucified under the public charge
made by the Romans that he was in fact seeking national
liberation—"This is Jesus, the King of the Jews"—and after Pilate had at the crowd's urging released a Zealot
leader, Barabbas, rather than Jesus.[26]

Given a sense of the revolutionary milieu and of Jesus'
own passion for justice, it is not difficult to feel the
reality of this temptation that he take up the sword
against the imperial forces and attempt to seize all power
for the people. But the prevailing argument in Jesus'

[26] Oscar Cullmann, "Jesus and the Resistance Movement of the Zealots," in The State in the New Testament (London, SCM Press: 1963),
pp. 14–24.

mind against Satan's offer is, in Luke's text, the very argument made by Satan himself: "I will give you all this power and the glory of these kingdoms, for it has been committed to me and I give it to anyone I choose. Worship me, then, and it shall all be yours" (Luke 4: 6–7). The power of these kingdoms, the power of the sword, belongs to Satan. To seize the sword and Caesar's power, for whatever end, is simply to worship Satan, and Jesus' reply is that God alone must be worshiped and served. For the sword of the world's kingdoms usurps the power of God, who alone has legitimate power over life and death. There is no kingdom and no state as defined by the sword which is not corrupted by Satan's condition for power. All have committed themselves to him, and so each is indicted by Jesus' challenge: that God alone deserves to be served.

The conclusion to this final drama in the desert, with Jesus' sweeping rejection of Caesar's power, is the most radical possible concerning the nature of God and the question of liberation. It becomes explicit in the verses in Luke following Jesus' return from the desert, when he goes into the synagogue in Nazareth on the sabbath and stands up to read Isaiah's text:

The spirit of the Lord has been given to me,
for he has anointed me.
He has sent me to bring the good news to the poor,
to proclaim liberty to captives
and to the blind new sight,
to set the downtrodden free,
to proclaim the Lord's year of favor.   (Luke 4:18–19; cf. Isa 61:1–2)

Jesus' comment on this proclamation of sweeping liberation to the poor, prisoners, the blind, and the oppressed, is a simple one; "This text is being fulfilled today even as you listen."

What are we to conclude from, first of all, Jesus' rejection in the desert of all the world's kingdoms and their power, past and future—and soon after his return from the desert, his identification of the Gospel with a proclamation of absolute freedom for all the world's oppressed peoples? The conclusion is that the God whom Jesus addresses so intimately as "*Abba*," and the inauguration of whose reign on earth is the core of Jesus' message, is a God of Liberation—and of such radical liberation that he wages a permanent revolution down through history against every kingdom and state in existence—a revolution to liberate *all* the oppressed, free *all* the prisoners, give back land to *all* the people—a revolution to set everyone free, to level all corporate and bureaucratic power, to break open the prisons, to smash every war machine known to man, and to do so without swearing allegiance to a single regime or ideology in history, for God the Liberator is alone to be worshiped, God the Condemned and Executed and Always Resurrected—the enemy of every state—is alone to be served.

But this is a Liberator God-Man whose suffering resistance puts the flame of truth to injustice only after man has first sought Him in silence in the heat of the desert and fought with his Spirit in the freezing wind of the mountain's dark side. In the desert, on the sheer face of the mountain, man becomes God by renouncing power and becoming nothing. Now yin, now yang, and for a few hours man is transfigured on the cross and resists with the power of God: The world changes.

The Liberator becomes man, and man the Liberator, when man has fallen freely to zero, for zero equals infin-

ity, and the Spirit is free at last to become a fire roaring
out of the one Reality—not man or God but the One, in
whom all are one, a single flame, burning suffering division into Being. The litany of the living-dying, dying-
living.

Resistance and contemplation, sunlight and darkness,
one Way, one God-man Liberator, a single roaring flame,
a question of Being: Just how far would we like to go
in?

THE REVOLUTION IS THE KINGDOM

In January 1971 Israeli archeologists discovered in a hill-
side cave near Jerusalem the first remains ever uncov-
ered of a victim of crucifixion. The bones of this man,
who judging from artifacts found in the tomb was probably executed by the Romans around A.D. 7, indicate
more precisely than was known before the way in which
another victim of Roman execution, Jesus of Nazareth,
died a quarter-century later:

> Once the victim's arms were immobilized, the Roman
> executioners most likely then turned to his legs, pressing
> them together and twisting them to one side, somewhat
> in the position of a deep-knee bend. Then the execu-
> tioners drove a large iron spike approximately 7 inches
> long through his two calcaneal (or heel) bones, and
> into the wood. To prevent the victim from sagging—
> and possibly tearing himself loose from the cross—a small
> crosspiece called a "sedecula" was nailed to the upright
> member of the cross; it provided a support shelf for
> the condemned man's buttocks. In most cases, the ex-
> perts think, death on the cross came within a span of
> several hours to a day or more, either from loss of blood
> or from suffocation as the victim's rib cage collapsed
> over his diaphragm.[1]

[1] "The Rite of Crucifixion," *Newsweek* (January 18, 1971), p. 53.

Jesus was executed in this way by the Roman State under the charge of sedition, a fact recorded in all four Gospels.[2] According to the more specific charges made against Jesus before Pilate by the chief priests and scribes, the grounds for his execution were: (1) inciting a revolution; (2) advocating tax resistance; (3) claiming authority to set up an alternate government to the State —"They began their accusation by saying, 'We found this man inciting our people to revolt, opposing payment of the tribute to Caesar, and claiming to be Christ, a king'" (Luke 23:2). A question worth reexamining in the light of today's political-spiritual challenges is what basis there was in reality for Jesus' execution as a revolutionary.

It has been suggested recently by S. G. F. Brandon in his important book *Jesus and the Zealots*[3] that Jesus was executed by the Romans because their Jewish collaborators sensed rightly that Jesus' proclaimed "kingdom" threatened the entire Roman-Jewish-upper-class power structure. Much of the chief priests' fear of Jesus' power arose from his assault, a few days before his execution, on the Temple trading system:

> So they reached Jerusalem and he went into the Temple and began driving out those who were selling and buying there; he upset the tables of the money changers and the chairs of those who were selling pigeons. Nor would he allow anyone to carry anything through the Temple. And he taught them and said, "Does not scripture say: 'My house will be called a house of prayer for all the peoples'? But you have turned it into a robbers' den." (Mark 11:15-17)

[2] Mark 15:1-2, 15-20, 26, 32; Matt. 27:11-31, 37; Luke 23:1-25, 36-38; John 18:29-19:24.

[3] S. G. F. Brandon, *Jesus and the Zealots* (Charles Scribner's Sons: 1967).

Mark's next sentence emphasizes the connection between this act of revolutionary non-violence and the steps leading to Jesus' execution: "This came to the ears of the chief priests and the scribes, and they tried to find some way of doing away with him; they were afraid of him because the people were carried away by his teaching."

They were afraid of him because *the people* were carried away by his teaching. Carried away to what?

Brandon suggests that Jesus' raid on the Temple was a symbolic takeover of the power of the sacerdotal government, which had made the organization and maintenance of the Temple into "an immense undertaking, involving enormous economic resources and the employment of a great body of officials and servants, control of which was lucrative and conferred great power and influence."[4] To make the point and introduce the specific focus of this essay, we can say that Jesus' attack on this trading system was no more a simple act of indignation directed against the sellers and money-changers employed at the bottom of the system than was the act of raiding a Catonsville, Maryland, draft office in May 1968 —by nine men and women, led by Fathers Daniel and Philip Berrigan—directed against the clerk-typists in the office. The target in both cases was an exploitative system, in particular the illegitimate authority of those controlling the system. However naïve the less-involved may wish to remain for their own sakes about the revolutionary non-violence of Jesus and the Catonsville Nine, the authorities in both cases realized the seriousness of the

[4] *Ibid.*, p. 331. See Brandon's fn. 5 *ad loc.* for articles documenting this point.

challenge (however much they misunderstood the nature of that challenge), and that Jesus and the Berrigan forces represented a fundamental threat to the security of the existing system. Those in power had to "find some way of doing away" with them—in Jesus' case, charges of armed insurrection resulting swiftly in his crucifixion; in the case of the Berrigans, who after their imprisonment continued by their example to give birth to a wider movement, charges of conspiracy to kidnap covering both them and a network of non-violent cadres so as to discredit publicly and tie up juridically a growing moral power.

The raid on the Temple trading system around A.D. 30 and the raid on the Catonsville draft office in 1968 were "symbolic" in the same explosive sense as was Mohandas Gandhi's beautifully illegal act in 1930 of bending over to pick up a handful of salt from the seashore: these actions were symbols of revolution, symbols of invitation to the people. The actions were living statements which invited the people to realize their own power, if they would only do likewise and act in concert. In Gandhi's case, in response to a brilliantly conceived and executed symbol of popular power, the people did act. Millions of Indian villagers began making salt in defiance of the British law against possessing salt not obtained from the government salt monopoly, and Britain's rule over India crumbled. In Jesus' case, with his Temple raid following shortly upon a triumphal entry into Jerusalem, the authorities sensed quickly the danger of a movement acting in concert with the Nazarean's attack on the system. Utilizing an easily manipulated judicial process, they had him killed. In the Berrigans' case, perhaps because nothing in mainstream American Catholicism had prepared them for it, the authorities were slower to recognize the significance of Catonsville.[5] But with the blooming of more and more Catonsvilles in 1968–70, with the targets widening from draft boards to the industrial side of the murderous complex (Dow Chemical and General Electric offices with defense contracts), and with support for the Berrigans growing in religious orders, in Middle America, and even in Congress, the government sensed suddenly the gathering power of the people through "symbolic" action. At the same time the FBI intercepted several letters which, if read apart from subsequent exchanges, it hoped would serve as the government's means of destroying the Berrigans' power.

The FBI sought to stifle the symbolic power of Catonsville and the Berrigans by making kidnaping charges based on an exchange of letters between Sister Elizabeth McAlister and Philip Berrigan which in themselves indicate, first, that the idea of a "non-violent kidnaping"—or citizen's arrest—of a government official was in fact discussed by McAlister and Berrigan, and secondly, that their discussion was riddled with confusion and contradictions. I believe these letters are strong evidence that Elizabeth McAlister and Philip Berrigan were fallible enough to consider taking an action which if thought through and carried out could hardly have avoided contradicting their commitment to non-violence. Yet there is no evidence—and I believe that the FBI knows and has known all along that there is no evidence—showing that they took concrete steps to do the action.[6] In short, to use

[5] If the authorities had been more familiar with Dorothy Day's Catholic Worker Movement, which has been nurturing Catholic revolutionaries since 1933, they would have been better prepared for Catonsville. *The Catholic Worker* is one of the first publications for which the Berrigans wrote on the issues of peace and racism.

[6] Thus I. F. Stone writes in his *Bi-Weekly* (May 17, 1971): "If one assumes the plot was abandoned, all the pieces of the government's puz-

a term which applies to Jesus and Gandhi as well as it does to McAlister and Berrigan, they were *tempted* to violate their calling. The fact that they refused that temptation is the reason why the U.S. government now finds it necessary to charge them not with any action but with temptation itself—which in the Justice Department is the de facto meaning of conspiracy. But if we are willing to judge men guilty for their temptations—in our courts or in our minds—then history is totally devoid of good men, and we the judges are the prisoners of our law.

The purpose of this essay is neither to defend the International Catholic Conspiracy which the United States government is seeking to expose nor to indict a government in turn which has already been judged beyond domestic repression and found genocidal. It is rather to reexamine that specific kind of revolution which centers itself on symbolic action at a time when following its burial by radical critics as an ineffective way to challenge institutional injustice, non-violent revolution has suddenly reemerged to provoke the most powerful government in history into a trial recalling that of Jesus. We should remember that the charge of sedition to violence

---

zling conduct begin to fit. It would explain why Hoover disclosed the plot instead of waiting to catch the plotters red-handed. It would also explain why the government released the letters with a new indictment instead of waiting to use them as key pieces of evidence in the trial. On trial, the letters would have had to be authenticated; the judge would rule on admissibility. They might look very differently in the full context of other evidence . . .

"Instead of waiting for a court ruling on these motions, the government jumped the gun by releasing these letters. This endangers their admissibility but serves the purpose of damaging all the defendants, though the letters would have been admissible if authenticated and in the event of severance only against those who wrote them. One can only conclude that this maneuver, like the attempt to peddle the documents to *Time* Magazine, indicates that the letters really wouldn't add up to much if subjected to fair trial procedures."

made against Jesus is one that the Gospels show he was unquestionably guilty of—if temptation by Satan (which must have meant a serious consideration by Jesus of that possible choice) is the measure of guilt. But the parallel of greater significance than the prophet's certain guilt as measured by his government is the parallel in symbolic actions which gave rise to such charges: Jesus in the Temple, the Berrigans at Catonsville.

The paradigm which throws light backward to the Temple and forward to Catonsville is that of Gandhi's Salt March. In terms of human consciousness, Gandhi's march may have been the most important political event to have taken place since Jesus' execution by the Romans, and the event which can in fact enable us to reenter Jesus' action in the Temple and its culmination on Golgotha. But we must first understand the background of Gandhi's march in India in 1930.[7]

The Salt March occurred in the context of a deepening mood of violence in India, and Gandhi's decision to undertake it was preceded by weeks of silent searching and agonizing. In December 1929, the British Viceroy in India, Lord Irwin, was almost killed on his way to a meeting with Gandhi when a bomb exploded under his train. The Indian National Congress, meeting a few days later, condemned the bombing but the resolution passed by only a narrow margin. The Congress then voted on New Year's Eve 1929 to proclaim complete independence from England to be India's goal, which (because of Gandhi's influence) would be sought through

[7] The books I have drawn upon for the details of the Salt March given here are: Geoffrey Ashe, *Gandhi* (Stein and Day: 1969); Louis Fischer, *The Life of Mahatma Gandhi* (Collier Books: 1962); Robert Payne, *The Life and Death of Mahatma Gandhi* (E. P. Dutton: 1969); Gene Sharp, *Gandhi Wields the Weapon of Moral Power: Three Case Histories* (Ahmedabad, Navajivan Publishing House: 1960).

a program of civil disobedience to British laws. The Congress gave Gandhi complete authority to determine the scope and timing of the campaign to free India.

During the first few weeks of 1930, Gandhi retreated into his ashram. He wrote in an article addressed "To English Friends" that "hatred and ill-will are undoubtedly in the air." He considered this danger an argument in favor of civil disobedience rather than against it, because inaction on his part would be an invitation to terrorists to take over the movement:

> The conviction has deepened in me that civil disobedience alone can stop the bursting of that fury. The nation wants to feel its power more even than to have independence. Possession of such power *is* independence . . .[8]

Nevertheless the civil disobedience to be undertaken had to be such as to, first, define the issues sharply, and secondly, keep the violence within India from erupting. When the great Indian poet Rabindranath Tagore visited Gandhi at the ashram on January 18, Gandhi told him, "I am furiously thinking night and day, and I do not see any light coming out of the surrounding darkness."[9]

As Gandhi continued through January and February to search inwardly for a clear program of action, his associates became disturbed. Nehru in particular became impatient with the prolonged silence. Then, in Gandhi's words, "like a flash it came, and as you know it was enough to shake the country from one end to the other."[10] Gandhi chose the Salt Act, which had set up a British government monopoly on the manufacture of salt

[8] Sharp, p. 52.
[9] Ashe, p. 282.
[10] Sharp, p. 56.

in India, as the issue on which to initiate the independence campaign. He proposed that Indians throw off the burden of the British by making their own salt.

The proposal prompted ridicule by the English and bewilderment among the intellectuals of the Indian Congress. But the issue was chosen by Gandhi for the people, who in a hot climate knew the heavy burden of a salt tax which cost a laborer with a family up to two weeks' wages a year. And the people responded.

In the early morning of March 12, 1930, a column of seventy-eight highly disciplined *satyagrahis* ("practitioners of truth-force," according to Gandhi's definition), emerged from the ashram onto a route to the sea lined by hundreds of thousands of Indians. The sixty-one-year-old Gandhi led them carrying a bamboo walking staff. "We are marching," he said, "in the name of God." The names of the volunteers for civil disobedience had been published in Gandhi's journal *Young India* for the benefit of the police. They walked twenty-four days on the dirt roads from village to village, 241 miles, until they reached Dandi on the coast, a shoreline where seawater evaporated on mudflats leaving a layer of salt. Gandhi had announced that he would then break the law by picking up some salt. His biographer Geoffrey Ashe describes the scene:

> On 5 April the marchers poured along the road with the sunset in their eyes. They camped near the water. Night fell and passed, and all through it the ashramites were praying . . . In the bright fresh minutes of the new morning, before its heat careered over the treetops, Gandhi waded into the ocean. From that huge and healing womb he presently turned back toward India, and paced over the sand to a spot where the salt lay thick. There he bent quickly over and scooped some of

it up with his fingers. Sarojini Naidu, who was among the pilgrims standing nearest, cried "Hail deliverer!" He straightened and held it out for all to see: the treasonable gift of God.[11]

The deliverance Gandhi initiated was a deliverance through prison. A month after the Dandi action at least 60,000 Indians had been jailed by the British for making salt. Millions more Indians continued to break the law. During the massive campaign, there was almost no Indian violence, and nowhere was there any violence by members of the Congress party, in spite of the police tactic of charging and beating crowds and in one case machine-gunning a crowd, killing seventy people. The people, in response to Gandhi's march and handful of salt, simply continued to make salt, to raid the British controlled salt works at the cost of hundreds of savagely beaten satyagrahis, and to defy the oppressor's law in every conceivable way without doing violence to him. They reduced the reign of imperial law to ruins. It was to be seventeen years of further conflict and civil disobedience campaigns before India was to gain her legal independence from Britain, but in the deepest sense possible, in the minds of the people, it was won when they recognized their freedom in the action of Gandhi bending over to pick up salt from the shore.

The Salt March was Gandhi's journey into the people. The symbolic gesture which climaxed it, igniting a power of resistance in the people setting them free and destroying British imperialism, was the conclusion of a contemplative journey which went deep enough to unite Gandhi with the people in the single reality of the Liberating God. Gandhi dropped into a silent void, "reduced

11 Ashe, p. 287.

himself to zero" in the Buddhist formula which he often repeated as the keynote for the man of non-violence, and found on the far side of nothingness the people, in whom God lived patiently, awaiting the full release of his unifying, liberating power. Gandhi dropped into the well of existence, where he could "not see any light coming out of the surrounding darkness," and there in deep solitude was given in a flash the symbol uniting darkness and light. Gandhi lost himself and found his life in the suffering of the people of God—all the people, Indian, British, all those whose inner life he felt and touched in darkness and in light, all of suffering mankind brought together for a moment in a handful of salt.

Gandhi's living definition of non-violent revolution was that it was an experiment in truth, truth being an unlimited spiritual power discoverable at that point where the depths of oneself passed over into the needs of a suffering people. The experiment in truth must therefore be conducted in a living laboratory of existence which spans personal and public life—one life, one truth, one Liberating Reality. The satyagrahi is a servant of God in the people. As a Gandhian disciple, Danilo Dolci, has said of the people he serves, "There is God in these people, like the fire that smolders under the ashes."[12] The satyagrahi in his experiment with truth must serve the people by helping to rekindle the fire under the ashes, the divine power of liberation within their suffering. By extinguishing his own desire for power, the satyagrahi seeks the authentic power of the people. He must discover in contemplation, and in the giving of his life, those symbolic actions which will ignite the people's faith to resist injustice with their whole lives,

[12] James McNeish, Fire Under the Ashes: The Life of Danilo Dolci (London, Hodder and Stoughton: 1965), p. 68.

lives coming together as a united force of truth and thus releasing the liberating power of the God within them.

Gandhi's program achieved independence for India because it was founded on the profoundly simple recognition that liberation always begins on the plot of ground where one stands. Swaraj, the Sanskrit term Indian politicians used for the independence they sought, meaning literally "one's own rule," was taken over by Gandhi in its political sense and integrated in all his campaigns with a personal, spiritual dimension which for the first time made every Indian conscious that he was responsible in the decisions of his own soul for the freedom of his country. Gandhi's favorite symbol of swaraj, personal and national, was the spinning wheel. If each Indian were to wear only cloth spun by his own hands, India's economic dependence on Britain's mills would cease. There could be no swaraj for India if Indians did not first choose swaraj for themselves. As Gandhi wrote in his widely circulated revolutionary pamphlet *Hind Swaraj:*

> . . . if we become free, India is free. And in this thought you have a definition of Swaraj. It is Swaraj when we learn to rule ourselves. It is, therefore, in the palm of our hands . . . such Swaraj has to be experienced, by each one for himself. One drowning man will never save another. Slaves ourselves, it would be a mere pretension to think of freeing others.[13]

The way to India's swaraj was therefore a constant increase of ever widening liberated zones: personal

[13] M. K. Gandhi, *Hind Swaraj*, in *The Selected Works of Mahatma Gandhi: Vol. IV*, ed. Shriman Narayan (Ahmedabad, Navajivan Publishing House: 1968), p. 155.

swaraj, communal swaraj, and ultimately national swaraj; freedom from the bondage of one's own self, freedom from such communal sins as untouchability and Hindu-Muslim hatred, freedom from British imperialism. If the people were to gain national independence, they would have to do so progressively through millions of smaller-scale struggles for freedom, out of which the nation's liberation would finally come as a matter of course. The British could not grant Indians swaraj. Indians had simply to choose it for themselves, compelling the British to acknowledge at some stage that their rule, whatever its sovereign claims, had in effect ceased to rule a people who had chosen to rule themselves.

The key to the entire program was the satyagrahi's —or non-violent resister's—own liberation, initiating a spiritual process which would end in national independence. Gandhi based his understanding of that liberation on Hinduism and the great Hindu scriptures, laying special stress on the teaching of the *Bhagavad-Gita* and the *Isha Upanishad.*

From the *Gita,* the supreme literary expression of Hinduism, Gandhi drew the theme of renunciation of the fruits of action as man's most perfect way to attain liberation. The problem which the *Gita* responds to is the classic Hindu identification of action with bondage to a lower self. Action, *karma,* kindles passion (the desire for one's own ends), thus binding man according to the law of karma more and more to the self-centered cycle of his own deeds. The most ancient Hindu response to the problem, proposed by the *Mundaka Upanishad,* was to recommend the extermination of action altogether. In order to attain liberation from the law of karma, and

realization of the Absolute, or *Brahman,* man had to renounce action and pursue a purely contemplative way
of life:

> Having scrutinized the worlds that are built up by work,
> a *brahmin* Should arrive at indifference. The [world]
> that was not made is not [won] by what is done.[14]

The *Gita,* however, distinguishes passion from action,
and defines a disciplined way of action—a way of dis-
passionate action by which man renounces the fruits,
ends, or rewards of his action—which will attain liberation and realization of the Absolute. The *Gita* dismisses
as unrealistic any hope of man's totally abstaining from
action, or work, and thus avoiding bondage to the self:
"For no one can remain even for a moment without
doing work; every one is made to act helplessly by the
impulses born of nature."[15] Action is unavoidable simply
by one's presence in the world, and he who seeks to
avoid it fails in his duty. The problem of liberation
therefore is not simply one of action but of *right* action,
and the *Gita* says action becomes liberation when one
has renounced its fruits. Action must become desireless,
selfless, detached—free of yearning for the fruits. Work
will be done according to one's duty, but at the center
of action, in the heart of man, all work must be purified
of any attachment to its ends. Thus the ancient tension
between binding action and liberating contemplation
is resolved in the *Gita* by making contemplation the
heart of action: "He who sees that the ways of renunciation and of action are one—he sees truly."[16] Renunciation

[14] *Mundaka Upanishad,* in *A Sourcebook in Indian Philosophy,* eds.
Sarvepalli Radhakrishnan and Charles A. Moore (Princeton University
Press: 1957), p. 52.
[15] *Bhagavad-gita,* in Radhakrishnan and Moore, p. 112.
[16] *Ibid.,* p. 120.

of the fruits of action, of one's own ends, is for the sake of concentrating one's active being totally upon union with Brahman: "Fix thy mind on Me; be devoted to Me; sacrifice to Me; prostrate thyself before Me; so shalt thou come to Me. I promise thee truly, for thou art dear to Me."[17]

The end of the *Gita's* active-contemplative way of renunciation, an end which Gandhi defined as the fullness of *satyagraha,* or truth-force, is the actor's final reduction to zero and disappearance into the gift of God Himself:

> The work of a man whose attachments are sundered, who is liberated, whose mind is firmly founded in wisdom, who does work as a sacrifice, is dissolved entirely. For him the act of offering is God; the oblation is God. By God is it offered into the fire of God. God is that which is to be attained by him who realizes God in his works.[18]

Gandhi found this same teaching of renunciation expressed in the first verse of the *Isha Upanishad,* which he translated as "The whole world is the garment of the Lord. Renounce it, then, and receive it back as the gift of God."[19] The world is God's. Man must therefore continually renounce the world because it is not his, and he may then enjoy it and work in it because God wishes him to become His active agent in the world's liberation from evil. But renunciation is not gained once and for all, "it is attainable only by a constant heart-churn," it is "a wrestling with death."[20]

17 *Ibid.,* p. 162.

18 *Ibid.,* p. 118.

19 In an interview with Vincent Sheean three nights before Gandhi was assassinated. Quoted in Sheean's book, *Lead, Kindly Light* (Random House: 1949), pp. 190–91.

20 M. K. Gandhi, *Hindu Dharma* (Ahmedabad, Navajivan Publishing House: 1950), p. 142.

Renunciation was the core of Gandhi's inner discipline, the heart of the doctrine of satyagraha. He was careful to define renunciation in a realistic way, and to show its harmony with the struggle for national liberation:

> Renunciation of fruit in no way means indifference to the result. In regard to every action one must know the result that is expected to follow, the means thereto, and the capacity for it. He, who, being thus equipped, is without desire for the result, and is yet wholly engrossed in the due fulfilment of the task before him, is said to have renounced the fruits of his action.[21]

Not only is renunciation of ends consistent with the goal of national liberation, it is the most effective means of attaining it:

> Again, let no one consider renunciation to mean want of fruit for the renouncer. The *Gita* reading does not warrant such a meaning. Renunciation means absence of hankering after fruit. As a matter of fact, he who renounces reaps a thousandfold.[22]

The point is that renunciation of the end of national liberation, a brooding over which will only result in frustration and violence or a loss of faith and nerve, frees one for total absorption into its means, a way of personal liberation embodied now fearlessly in one's own life and action. And in turn, the end of national liberation draws that much closer as its agents renounce it as a distant ideological goal in order to embrace it as a personal way of life: a liberated people is created through the determined work and expanding power of liberated persons. The key to the people's liberation is the satyagrahi's liberation, whose center is renunciation.

21 *Ibid.*, p. 143.
22 *Loc. cit.*

The ever expanding power of satyagraha liberation is evident in the Salt March and its final, explosive symbolic action. In the preparatory weeks of withdrawal and silence, the satyagrahi, Gandhi, experienced darkness, powerlessness, no way out. According to the inner discipline he has given us, he must at that time have renounced all ends as defined by himself, falling for weeks into the utter desolation of complete powerlessness while Congress leaders demanded with increasing urgency that he act. To remain utterly still and concentrated, in a climate of violence, bitterness, and ringing demands for action, was Gandhi's way of revolution, and the source of his resulting action's enormous power when it was finally undertaken. The flash of light—the issue: salt —the symbol; a hand lifting salt from the shore, lawbreaking by fingering God's gift—illuminated Gandhi, but it dismayed Congress intellectuals. The people understood because the satyagrahi's journey into powerlessness had taken him finally into the powerlessness of the people, and at that point where zero becomes infinity, made him choose their issue and their symbol.

Gandhi shows the satyagrahi to be a priest symbolizing the kingdom, discovering in contemplation a sacrament of action which will announce to the people that the power and the kingdom are theirs, if they will only realize their freedom. The satyagrahi doesn't try to give power to the people, nor does he seek power for them. He helps to release the power that is already in the people. The people have the power within to liberate themselves. They need only realize this divine power. It is the satyagrahi's task to help them realize it by giving it symbolic expression. The satyagrahi's symbol is the sacrament of the revolution, at which point the people come together in a new understanding of the liberation lying within and among them. Gandhi helped the people make India's revolution by giving them a handful of salt and a spinning wheel. What he really gave them was an understanding of their own power of liberation.

The people's power of liberation is a divine power because the satyagrahi seeks with his symbol an awakening of power in *all* the people. His act of sacrifice is a statement of freedom addressed first to the oppressed, because they are first in the order of suffering, and in the need for liberation. But it is also addressed beyond the oppressed to the oppressors, and beyond them to all the world's people, who stand always in need of further liberation through the example of God's truthful, loving presence in man. When Gandhi was asked at Dandi what he hoped to accomplish by breaking the salt laws, he answered, "I want world sympathy in this battle of Right against Might," and he wrote out the words in unusually vigorous handwriting.[23] Gandhi's faith in truth as a liberating power ("Truth is God") was a faith also in the people, all the people, a faith that world sympathy would in fact be moved deeply enough by the suffering truth of India's millions in revolution to exercise a decisive effect upon British policies. He was right. World opinion united behind the independence struggle after it witnessed the disciplined nonviolence of Indian law-breakers in 1930, in sharp contrast to the savage police charges ordered by the British. Thus the human family as a whole became a bearer of that divine power of truth which had received its most universal expression in Gandhi's gesture by the

[23] Payne, p. 392.

sea. Gandhi's symbol of revolt could speak to everyone. It was a symbol drawn from the waters which washed up on all the shores of the world's oceans. After Gandhi's symbol broke into the human conscience, any man could understand the tyranny of British law in India by letting seawater run through his fingers.

"My house will be called a house of prayer *for all the peoples*," said Jesus quoting Isaiah after he had disrupted the Temple trading system, "But you have turned it into a robbers' den." Gandhi offered his symbol of revolt for all the people by the sea, and Jesus offered his in the Temple.

The traders whom Jesus drove out of the Temple were, as we saw, simply the lowest echelon of an established system of revenue controlled by the chief priests. Not only was the Temple trading system a means of exploiting the Jewish people for the benefit of a small priestly class, but it was also a part of the Roman power structure. Jesus' attack on the Temple trading system was a revolutionary act because

> the high priest held his office and authority from the Romans, and was thus an essential factor of the Roman government in Judaea. To challenge the rule of the high priest was thus, in effect, to challenge the Roman rule.[24]

[24] Brandon, p. 332. Although the Gospels present the top of this power structure, Pilate, as being opposed to Jesus' crucifixion, John's account (which is most sympathetic to Pilate) mentions that the arrest of Jesus was carried out by "the cohort together with a detachment of guards sent by the chief priests and the Pharisees" (John 18:3). The "cohort" refers to a detachment from the Roman garrison in Jerusalem, thus indicating from the time of the decision to arrest Jesus close collaboration between chief priests and Romans. Haim Cohn writes in *The Trial and Death of Jesus* (Harper and Row: 1971): "The Johannine version that Jesus was arrested by the whole or a part of a Roman cohort, commanded by its tribune, with the Jewish temple police and its commanding officer in attendance, is now being accepted as the true statement of facts by most contemporary scholars" (p. 78).

Jesus disrupted this entrenched "robbers'" system of chief priests and Roman rulers in the name of Yahweh's identification of the Temple with a universal brotherhood in prayer: "a house of prayer for all the peoples." In this connection, the New Testament scholar G. H. C. Macgregor has pointed out, "Probably the scene of the desecration [by the traders] was the outer Court, which was open to Gentiles. The foreigner was being robbed of his right to approach to Israel's God."[25]

After driving out the traders, Jesus initiated a daily teaching presence of his own in the Temple (Luke 19:47). This assumption of authority by Jesus, supported by the people who "hung on his words" (Luke 19:48), so alarmed the chief priests and scribes that they began to plot his death. They recognized that the Temple cleansing by Jesus had been a symbolic takeover of power by one who claimed to represent in God's name all the people. The prophetic symbol of Jesus' claim—a messianic figure whipping cattle and sheep panic-stricken from the Court, knocking over traders' tables, scattering cash left and right (John 2:15–16)—offered no hope that he could be bought off by the power structure. Most important, "they were afraid of him because the people were carried away by his teaching." So they "tried to find some way of doing away with him," and with the cooperation of the Roman authorities, succeeded in having Jesus executed for sedition: "We found this man inciting our people to revolt, opposing payment of the tribute to Caesar, and claiming to be Christ, a king (Luke 23:2)."[26]

[25] G. H. C. Macgregor, *The New Testament Basis of Pacifism* (Fellowship Publications: 1960), p. 18.

[26] I take up here only the first and broadest of the three charges against Jesus (though indicating a position on the third): that Jesus incited the

In what sense was Jesus' symbol of revolt an invitation to the people to do likewise? To what extent did he in fact represent a threat to the authority of chief priests and Romans?

S. G. F. Brandon's exhaustive effort to answer this question, through a study of Jesus' relation to the violent revolutionary movement of the Zealots (two of whom were probably crucified on his left and right), amounts to an ingenious second-guessing of the sources with no direct evidence for an answer, although his study is valuable in deepening our awareness that Jesus lived and died in an intensely revolutionary social climate. Brandon's own predisposition to identify Jesus as a Zealot mainly from the Gospel accounts of the Temple raid, and against the weight of Jesus' Gospel teaching, derives from his inability to distinguish militant non-violence from armed insurrection.[27] But a text which appears in

---

people to revolt. The second is discussed briefly in *The Non-Violent Cross*, pp. 189–90, but at the time of writing it I was without the benefit of Brandon's work which is especially helpful in understanding the Zealot background for Jesus' statement on paying tribute to Caesar. I now believe that Brandon's judgment that Jesus could not have been indifferent to the question of Jewish liberation is closer to the truth than Father John L. McKenzie's view that Rome was simply "trivial" in the light of the Gospels. In the sense of faith's living and enduring in any political context and ultimately transcending it, McKenzie is right, but this view taken by itself says too little about the Gospel's response to injustice and to the specific suffering of one's brothers. For the views of two scholars familiar with the Zealot background who discuss all three charges against Jesus and reach conflicting conclusions, see Brandon, pp. 322–58, and Oscar Cullmann, *The State in the New Testament* (London, SCM Press: 1963), pp. 14–42.

[27] Brandon asserts that Jesus' "recorded sayings and actions signify variously both pacifism and violence" (p. 20). But over against the extensive evidence for pacifism, he cites as "violent" only the two versions (Matt. 10:34 f.; Luke 12:51 f.) of Jesus' saying that he has come to earth not to bring peace but a sword of division (which Brandon understands, against the text, in a physical sense), Luke 22:36, "if you have no sword, sell your cloak and buy one" (a puzzling statement by Jesus but

the course of his investigation, from Josephus' *Jewish War*, in fact indicates another possibility (though Brandon fails to note it), since it shows that Jesus' people were familiar with a form of resistance to illegitimate authority which would be described today as "massive non-violent direct action."

Josephus relates that some time during the reign of the fifth procurator of Judaea, Pontius Pilate (A.D. 26–36), an uprising of the people against Roman rule occurred which ended in a dramatic demonstration of non-violent power and Pilate's retreat on a significant issue:

> Pilate, sent by Tiberius as procurator to Judaea, secretly and under cover of night brought into Jerusalem the images of Caesar known as standards. This act, when day broke, engendered a fearful tumult among the Jews; those close to the standards were seized with dismay, their laws, as it were, being trampled underfoot, for these laws permitted no image to be placed in the city. The city's indignant crowds were augmented by vast multitudes pouring in from the countryside. Hastening to Pilate at Caesarea, they implored him to remove the standards from Jerusalem and to preserve their ancestral laws. When Pilate rejected their pleas, they fell prostrate on the ground and stayed so for five days and nights.

one which nevertheless has a non-violent exegesis built into it in his next phrase referring to the necessary fulfillment of a scriptural prophecy and his abrupt termination of the conversation when the apostles take him literally), and the four accounts of the cleansing of the Temple (whose most obvious interpretation today as militant non-violence Brandon seems not even to have considered). The primary difficulty here, I believe, is Brandon's unquestioning choice of "pacifism" as the opposite of violence, and a concept which he is right in having difficulty applying to actions and attitudes of Jesus which deserve a more aggressive yet non-lethal description. *Jesus and the Zealots* might have been written with a further, necessary dimension had Brandon been as familiar with non-violence as he was with the British Army, which he served in as a chaplain for twelve years.

On the following day Pilate ascended his tribunal in the great circus and summoned the people, as if to give them the answer they craved; then he gave a prearranged signal to a body of armed troops to surround the Jews. Encircled by three-deep rings of soldiers, the Jews were dumbfounded at the unexpected sight. Pilate, declaring that he would cut them down if they refused to admit the standards of Caesar, signaled to the soldiers to draw their swords. As if by preconcerted agreement, the Jews fell prostrate in a mass, and offering their necks, cried that they would rather die than transgress the law. Amazed at the force of their devotion to their religion, Pilate ordered the immediate removal of the standards from Jerusalem. (*War* II 9:2–3)[28]

Josephus gives no details of how this mass movement was organized and led on its sixty-mile march from Jerusalem to Caesarea and during the subsequent six-day demonstration. Nor does he identify any Jewish spokesmen with the petition to Pilate that the Roman standards be removed. But the disciplined spirit of non-violence indicates Jewish revolutionary leadership of a non-Zealot kind, and the massive size of such a movement shows the people's readiness to engage in large-scale direct action. Without falling into Brandon's tendency to construct a revolutionary scenario for the Gospel by second-guessing the sources (whether on the side of violence or non-violence), we can at least understand why Jesus' attack on the trading system, occurring in such a context, so alarmed the chief priests collaborating with the Romans: "They were afraid of him because the people were carried away by his teaching." If the people had already been carried away (by someone) into a massive sixty-mile march and demonstration which had

[28] Nahum N. Glatzer, ed., *Jerusalem and Rome: The Writings of Josephus* (Meridian Books: 1960), pp. 144–45.

forced Pilate to remove the Roman standards from Jerusalem, the chief priests had reason to fear Jesus' challenge to their Roman-based authority. Coming as it did (according to the Synoptic Gospels' chronology) several hours after the people's acclamation of Jesus as the Messiah during his triumphal entry into Jerusalem,[29] the symbolic takeover of the Temple was a revolutionary act of the first order—that order being the consciousness of the people that the present system of power was coming radically into question.

For Jesus the basis of that question, the revolutionary reality, was the kingdom: "Set your hearts on [the Father's] kingdom first, and on his righteousness, and all these other things will be given you as well. So do not worry about tomorrow: tomorrow will take care of itself" (Matt. 6:33).[30]

The Zealot-Roman conflict was a conflict about tomorrow: whether tomorrow's state in Israel would be governed by nationalist Jews or imperialist Romans.

[29] Matthew and Luke describe the Temple action as following immediately on the Triumphal Entry (Matt. 21:10–12; Luke 19:41–45), while Mark has it occurring on the following day (Mark 11:11–12, 15).

[30] For the kind of exegesis employed here—applying to the question of one's attitude toward state power a command found originally in a discourse on Providence—see Robert C. Tannehill's article, "The 'Focal Instance' as a Form of New Testament Speech: A Study of Matthew 5:39b–42," *The Journal of Religion* (October 1970), pp. 372–85. The "focal instance" is a mode of language (usually a command), used frequently by Jesus in the synoptic tradition, which is deliberately open-ended: "Because it is extreme, the command indirectly refers to everything up to and including the literal sense. Thus the limits of the literal sense of the words have been broken down. It is not 'just that' which is commanded but 'even that.' And so the command acquires a whole field of implications to which no clear limits can be set" (p. 380). Just as a command dealing explicitly with a slap on the right cheek, Tannehill's example can only have been meant to produce an imaginative shock in the serious hearer, enabling him to see *his own* situation in a new way against his natural tendency to self-protection, so also with regard to letting tomorrow's needs of food and clothing take care of themselves while setting one's heart on the kingdom—and an oppressed people's natural tendency to attempt to seize state power.

Jesus' conflict with the ruling class of chief priests was not over the specific identity—Jew or Roman—of those who would exercise tomorrow's power over other men. Jesus' conflict was with the very kind of power which would subject *any* man to the control and violence of another, for whatever self-defined reason, classist, imperialist, or nationalist. "My house will be called a house of prayer for all the peoples."

Like the Zealots, Jesus recognized the imperative of resistance to injustice for the man of truth, and he repeatedly warned his disciples of the personal cost of truth in their mission. Jesus insisted on the primary need for *metanoia,* telling anyone wishing to be His disciple that he would have to renounce himself, take up his cross, and be prepared to face execution.

But for Jesus like Gandhi (who looked to Jesus as a model for the satyagrahi), the way of renunciation was for the sake of the kingdom, which is not tomorrow's national objective but a constant personal and communal possibility. The kingdom is already present: "The coming of the kingdom of God does not admit of observation and there will be no one to say, 'Look here! Look there!' For, you must know, the kingdom of God is among you" (Luke 17:20-21). Which is no more to say that Jesus' kingdom was indifferent to the just political goal of Jewish liberation from Rome than Gandhi's swaraj was to Indian liberation from England. Jesus' symbolic takeover of the Temple, like Gandhi's Salt March, was on one level an open invitation to revolt and an undermining of the existing power structure in the minds of the people. Had the Jewish people chosen to imitate Jesus' way of symbolic revolution rather than the Zealots' way of arms, instead of being overrun by the Romans in A.D. 66–70 they might have achieved a non-violent victory over the Empire analogous to that of the early Christian Church (before it, too, turned to armed power and used it especially to persecute an exiled Zion).

But again on a deeper level, the takeover of the Temple, the execution on the cross that followed, and the proclamation "He is risen!" announced in the most powerful symbolism mankind has known a new kind of revolution and liberation. It is a liberation which has been distorted, profaned, and obscured by church and state almost since its announcement but which nevertheless in the Gospel continues to inspire men of truth to a revolutionary commitment, and which may now, in an age of global exploitation, be awaiting a rediscovery which would shake the world's ruling powers to their foundations. When Jesus took over the Temple in the name of the people of God, all the earth's peoples, he stated in the language of revolution, in action, the political meaning of the Gospel: that the God of Love and Truth commands us to break down every division within and among ourselves and to create from the mass of mankind a new and more fully human community. The Gospel commandment of liberation permits no compromise, not the compromise of established injustice which would delay action until tomorrow: For you must set your hearts first on the kingdom, it is already among you, take up your cross. Nor does the Gospel commandment of liberation permit the compromise of sectarian violence and power-seeking: For the kingdom is given to the poor in spirit, not the power-seekers but the meek inherit the earth. The Gospel of Liberation commands man to act, to revolt against inhumanity, but to do so along a narrow way of renunciation on which the primary act

is the satyagrahi's silent revolution in the desert of re-
jecting the satanic temptation and renouncing every
claim to power—renouncing the fruits—thus freeing him
to enter and proclaim the kingdom which is close at
hand. "Repent, and believe the good news."

The good news of Catonsville: How to believe it?
I read the news early on the morning after it happened,
standing beside a newspaper vendor at a corner of the
University of Hawaii campus. How to believe—to enter
into—the reality of liberation described on the front page
in terms of nine men and women, good friends among
them, openly destroying with napalm the deadly paper
of Selective Service files? How to believe in the good
news of men and women burning paper rather than
children? What does one do with the Gospel when it
comes in the front door? Have a chair, Phil. Sit down,
Dan. Sorry, we've just been to Catonsville, on our way
to jail now. See you there?

Catonsville, like Jesus in the Temple and Gandhi
by the sea, was an invitation to faithful action. It was
an invitation to put away fear and join in breaking
open a house of prayer for all the peoples: to contemplate
the symbol—feel the living faith—be moved along one's
own way to the kingdom of resistance and liberation.

The deeper power of Catonsville, what compelled a
personal response, was the symbol's communion (because of the participants' communion) with the people
and their reality: a burning people, a homeless people,
a crater-pocked land with napalmed children. Dan
Berrigan had gone to the depths of Hanoi, sharing a
bomb shelter with Vietnamese children while American
planes roared overhead, and Phil Berrigan had experienced communion with the people in a black ghetto

which spoke of the suffering of all the world's exploited. Phil had also experienced the darkness of abandonment by the American peace movement during the months in prison after his first major act of civil disobedience in the fall of 1967, when his conscience-jarring act of pouring blood on draft files had been supported by almost no one. (Perhaps that cell of abandonment— the even more radical resolution given in it—was the primary factor in the power of Catonsville the following spring.) Each of the nine had in some way shared personally the suffering and powerlessness of the people. Together they knew the action needed to convey the people's reality, and as a symbol, napalm employed by the clergy at Catonsville carried a shock *capable* of breaking through American defenses with the suffering of the Vietnamese people. But in the months following the Catonsville action, Americans seemed to live more easily with bombs burning children than they could with priests burning paper. The nine at Catonsville extended a symbolic invitation which for a while seemed destined to become a judgment upon America by the God who suffers and dies in the midst of the people awaiting a response to his kingdom: "The kingdom of heaven is like a dragnet cast into the sea that brings in a haul of all kinds. When it is full, the fishermen haul it ashore; then, sitting down, they collect the good ones in a basket and throw away those that are no use" (Matt. 13:47–48).

But the kingdom is also like the mustard seed sown in the field, the smallest of all the seeds, which grows into the tree "so that the birds of the air come and shelter in its branches" (Matt. 13:32). The seed sown at Catonsville grew slowly and began to burst into view in Milwaukee, Chicago, Washington; in scores of draft-board and industrial-complex raids led in large part by Catholic radicals. The seed of Catonsville grew in the minds and hearts of students, Blacks, Chicanos, the powerless, who recognized it as a rare summons to freedom in a time of oppression and desperation. The seed grew in Dan and Phil Berrigan's Jesuit and Josephite brothers, and in other religious orders, with increasing numbers of clergy and sisters finding themselves in joyful jeopardy with the law. The seed grew in another new breeding ground for revolution, in the homes of middle-class Americans who sheltered Dan Berrigan during his four months of underground activity while the FBI sought him. The seed even grew in the media, which finally began to note that something prophetic rather than simply grotesque may have taken place at Catonsville. And the seed grew in Congress, in Senator Charles Goodell who at the possible cost of his Senate seat succeeded in having the Bureau of Prisons remove Phil Berrigan from a brutal maximum security confinement, and it grew in the conscience of Representative William R. Anderson who denounced J. Edgar Hoover for proclaiming the Berrigans guilty without trial. Because of the growing mustard seed which was becoming a tree and already beginning to shelter a large and varied population of birds, because the Berrigans refused to leave the people and come quietly, because they resisted to the point of discrediting the powers, the United States government tried to find some way of doing away with them. And it may succeed unless it becomes clear to the people, in America as well as Indochina, who is on trial.

The revolution is the kingdom because the revolution is the people coming together in a new humanity, ignited by a divine symbol given through the man of truth—Jesus in the Temple and on the cross, Gandhi by the sea, the Berrigans at Catonsville. The revolution is the kingdom among us realized by those who renounce the fruits, surrender to darkness and silence, and experience the suffering of the people and the power of the living God. The revolution is the kingdom conceived in contemplation and born into the world in resistance. The revolution is the kingdom of man liberated finally by the God already present in him.

PSYCHEDELIC CONTEMPLATION

For many Americans seeking freedom from the technological society, the logic for psychedelic contemplation as their way of liberation has seemed obvious: the technological society imposes on its members an environment of rationalism, materialism, and machinery which fragments and cripples the human personality. Psychedelic drugs, on the other hand, expand a crippled consciousness into the luminous experience of a single, all-embracing reality, whose transcendence to American society for the suddenly liberated head needs no argument.

Experimenters in LSD, mescaline, and related hallucinogenic drugs often claim that psychedelics possess a liberating power socially as well as psychically. One writer sympathetic to the counter-culture expresses a popular underground view when he asserts that the use of such drugs is revolutionary:

> The drug revolution is probably the most frontal assault that could be made on a society.
> Simply, a great number of young middle-class whites hate the "self" that their society has given them . . .
> What the drug revolution is really all about is the

fact that many middle-class youngsters cannot stand being in a social mansion surrounded by a global ghetto.

And so what they do is attack themselves.

They bomb themselves with drugs. They corrode their
egos with acid.[1]

The conclusion is that "since one is programmed by
society," "then any massive assault on one's inherited
self is an attack on society."

That psychedelic drugs are the means to a spiritual
revolution is a counter-culture conviction pervasive
enough to deserve critical attention. The attention given
psychedelic drugs here will be from the standpoint of
the question: How should such drugs be evaluated
within the yin-yang dynamism of revolutionary change,
contemplation-resistance-liberation? Does psychedelic
contemplation reissue into the world in resistance, as
Mohandas Gandhi's and Thomas Merton's contemplative lives did, and as any twentieth-century contemplative's life must in an age of global injustice and violence?
Does psychedelic contemplation free one to become a
liberating force for others? Just as Dietrich Bonhoeffer
in his prison cell in Nazi Germany described Jesus as
"the man for others," so can we describe the contemplative life today as "liberation for others," the liberation
of oneself through the pure gift of the Father, and that
liberated life put to the service of all men's liberation—
through a resistance to the "principalities and powers"
which Paul referred to in his letters to the early Christian communities and which in the twentieth century
take the form of war, racism, and global exploitation.
In this yin-yang of resistance and contemplation, how
are we to evaluate the liberating power of psychedelics?

If the logic for psychedelic drugs were joined to the

[1] Bob Hunter in his Vancouver *Sun* column, March 6, 1971.

argument of this book, it would say: Liberation into a genuine human freedom demands resistance to totalitarian institutions. Resistance in turn demands the divine base of contemplation, an experience of the One, to be able to hold its ground against institutional murder. But given the imminent threats of nuclear war, global famine, and ecological disaster, the time to realize such a visionary experience for any significant number of men is short. Moreover, Western man, in the saddle of a runaway technology and in desperate need of a contemplative center, is cut off from the ascetic disciplines and mainly Eastern sources which have been the traditional way to that experience. Therefore the appearance of easily accessible psychedelic drugs at man's most threatening moment in history can be hailed as a providential means of providing him this unitive experience, which can then serve as the basis for man's, especially Western man's, liberation.

Dr. Timothy Leary, the most widely known advocate of psychedelic contemplation, has summarized the value of mind-expanding drugs in the paradox: "it becomes necessary for us to go out of our minds in order to use our heads."[2] He argues that religious believers in particular should welcome a pharmacological means of ensuring ecstasy:

> We recall that most of the great religions have taken this goal, *ex-stasis*, the going beyond the rational, as their central program. The fact that we now possess the chemical means for guaranteeing this process should be a cause for rejoicing—for those who take their religion or their neurology seriously.[3]

[2] Timothy Leary, Introduction to *LSD: The Consciousness-Expanding Drug*, edited by David Solomon (Berkeley Medallion: 1966), p. 13.
[3] *Ibid.*, p. 25.

Leary's former associate, Dr. Richard Alpert, states what this means to the Western seeker of liberation:

> The Westerner is not prepared to undertake a discipline which one must pursue for many years on faith and with a low likelihood of success. Thus other more dramatic ways, such as the use of external chemical agents as catalysts, lend themselves more to his disposition. In but a brief hour he can achieve states of transcendence for which an Easterner must spend years (assuming, as many reporters do, that the two experiences are somewhat comparable, at least in certain aspects).[4]

For critics inclined on the contrary to dismiss quickly any suggestion of similarity between chemical and non-chemical transcendental states, Dr. Husten Smith, one of the most respected scholars of comparative religion and no LSD publicist, has suggested caution and a basic respect for the testimony of others. Smith believes that, *viewed phenomenologically,* psychedelic experiences and mystical experiences cannot be distinguished. He cites several studies which reach this conclusion through different routes and quotes the current philosophical authority on mysticism, Dr. W. T. Stace, saying of the drug experience: "It's not a matter of its being *similar* to mystical experience; it *is* mystical experience. . . ."[5] (Stace's emphasis.)

Dr. Allan Y. Cohen, a psychologist involved earlier as a student in Leary's and Alpert's ground-breaking experiments in LSD at Harvard and who now takes a sharply critical view of such drugs, also believes that

[4] Richard Alpert and Sidney Cohen, *LSD* (New American Library: 1966), p. 56.
[5] Huston Smith, "Do Drugs Have Religious Import?", in *LSD: The Consciousness-Expanding Drug*, p. 162.

the psychedelic experience as a phenomenon is indistinguishable from a religious experience:

> The experience under these materials was sufficiently dramatic that, with the proper set and settings, you could be 100% sure that you had experienced God. But the question which had to be faced was: *did* you experience God? There is no question that chemicals, and other forms of external manipulation like fasting and flagellation, can produce alterations of consciousness and religious experiences. If I stick you in a church and give you 500 micrograms of LSD I will guarantee you a religious experience.[6]

Because they see the psychedelic experience as a phenomenon corresponding to mystical experiences, Allan Cohen and Huston Smith are not for that reason prepared to embrace psychedelics as a new faith. They simply believe that the important distinction to be made is not between drug and religious experiences, but between the phenomenon of religious experiences (however induced) and the more deeply significant reality of religious life as a whole. As Smith says: "Drugs appear able to induce religious experiences; it is less evident that they can produce religious lives."[7]

Although Leary and Alpert have been the publicists of psychedelics, the two writers who have probably argued the case for psychedelic contemplation most persuasively have been Aldous Huxley, who experimented with the drugs up until his death, and Alan Watts, whose "adventures in the chemistry of consciousness" provided the text for his popular book, *The Joyous Cosmology*. It is Huxley who in his last book, *Island*, presented what

[6] Allan Y. Cohen, "LSD and the Search for God" (*The Catonsville Roadrunner:* Issue No. 20).
[7] Smith, p. 167.

Richard Alpert believes is "one of best descriptions of a model for a culture in which the psychedelic experience plays a crucial role."[8] And it is Watts who, according to Leary and Alpert in their foreword to *The Joyous Cosmology*, "has given us perhaps the best statement on the subject of space-age mysticism . . . Watts follows Mr. Huxley's lead and pushes beyond."[9] *Island* and *The Joyous Cosmology* can serve here as two classic statements of psychedelic contemplation to be examined critically in the light of the yin-yang way of liberation.

Island is Huxley's vision of a utopia created largely through the systematic use of hallucinogenic drugs. In his novel he shows the inhabitants of the cloistered island Pala being liberated from murderous creeds by the periodic use, beginning in adolescence, of drugs known as "*moksha*-medicine." As a member of Palan society explains to Will Farnaby, a journalist shipwrecked on its shore: "with four hundred milligrams of *moksha*-medicine in their bloodstreams, even beginners . . . can catch a glimpse of the world as it looks to someone who has been liberated from his bondage to the ego."[10]

Pala's century-old freedom from technology and materialism is threatened by the greed, virtually unique to the island, of its young prince, Murugan. According to the spiritual head of Pala, Dr. Robert McPhail, the prince's drive to overrun the island with technology, symbolized by his fascination with motor scooters, is the result of Western miseducation and his Puritanic refusal to take the *moksha*-medicine:

8 Alpert and Cohen, p. 67.
9 Timothy Leary and Richard Alpert, Foreword to *The Joyous Cosmology*, by Alan Watts (Vintage Books: 1962), p. xiv.
10 Aldous Huxley, *Island* (Bantam Books: 1963), p. 139.

". . . he hasn't learned, and doesn't want to learn, the easy way."

"Which is the easy way?" Will asked.

"Education and reality-revealers. Murugan has had neither. Or rather he's had the opposite of both. He's had miseducation in Europe—Swiss governesses, English tutors, American movies, everybody's advertisements—and he's had reality eclipsed for him by his mother's brand of spirituality. So it's no wonder he pines for scooters."[11]

Murugan's subjects, however, according to Dr. McPhail, have been fully liberated from the technological society by education and *moksha*-medicine, or "reality-revealers":

"They've been taught from infancy to be fully aware of the world, and to enjoy their awareness. And, on top of that, they have been shown the world and themselves and other people as these are illumined and transfigured by reality-revealers. Which helps them, of course, to have an intenser awareness and a more understanding enjoyment, so that the most ordinary things, the most trivial events, are seen as jewels and miracles. Jewels and miracles," he repeated emphatically. "So why should we resort to scooters or whisky or television or Billy Graham or any other of your distractions and compensations?"[12]

Moksha-medicine versus motor scooters, psychedelics against the technological society, is a polarity which needs to be examined carefully in the light of a critical understanding of technique. For that we must consider for a moment the nature of technique itself before returning to Huxley's psychedelic utopia.

"Technique" is the term used by Jacques Ellul in his

[11] *Ibid.*, p. 143.
[12] *Ibid.*, pp. 143–44.

work *The Technological Society,* the most important study of this phenomenon, to describe the environment which now encloses almost all modern communities after the effects of industrialism, science, and the media. We have all become creatures of technique. Technique is "the totality of methods rationally arrived at and having absolute efficiency (for a given stage of development) in every field of human activity."[13] Technique is not only the machinery we use. It is the state of mind which uses us. Technique is the new environment of man which has replaced nature. It is an environment in which mechanics have been brought to bear on all that is spontaneous or irrational, and in which the overriding criterion of all planning and action is efficiency. As creatures of technique, we do not ask, "Is it right to do?" Or, "Is it wise?" We ask rather, "Does it work?" "Is it effective?"

The war in Indochina illustrates the characteristics of a society dominated by the technique which Aldous Huxley's island society claims to have left behind. As a proving ground for war, Indochina is the answer to the American technician's dream. Pentagon technicians can experiment almost endlessly to learn the efficiency of every new explosive device off the assembly line in the ideal laboratory of Southeast Asian insurrection, where most of the suffering is remote, un-American, and can be written off. What works? Try this and this. Measure the results: body counts, captured supplies, telltale enemy actions. If that doesn't work, choose from a thousand more possibilities being produced by technicians at their

[13] Jacques Ellul, *The Technological Society* (Alfred A. Knopf: 1965), p. xxv. An excellent essay on Ellul which has been helpful in preparing the following analysis is James Y. Holloway's "West of Eden" (*Katallagete:* Winter/Spring 1970), pp. 6–15. The same essay is in *Introducing Jacques Ellul,* edited by Holloway (William Eerdmans: 1970).

drawing boards and by an industrial complex ever ready to turn killing concepts into reality. Try it all out in Southeast Asia. Discover what works.

Thus General Westmoreland, in a 1969 speech quoted by Noam Chomsky in *At War with Asia,* believes that "technologically the Vietnam war has been a great success." General Westmoreland "sees machines carrying more and more of the burden." He says:

> I see an army built into and around an integrated area control system that exploits the advanced technology of communications, sensors, fire direction, and the required automatic data processing—a system that is sensitive to the dynamics of the ever-changing battlefield—a system that materially assists the tactical commander in making sound and timely decisions.[14]

A vision of further technological success is presented by Leonard Sullivan, Deputy Director of Research and Development for Southeast Asian Matters:

> These developments open up some very exciting horizons as to what we can do five or ten years from now: When one realizes that we can detect anything that perspires, moves, carries metal, makes a noise, or is hotter or colder than its surroundings, one begins to see the potential. This is the beginning of instrumentation of the entire battlefield. Eventually, we will be able to tell when anybody shoots, what he is shooting at, and where he was shooting from. You begin to get a "Year 2000" vision of an electronic map with little lights that flash for different kinds of activity. This is what we require for this "porous" war, where the friendly and the enemy are all mixed together.[15]

[14] Noam Chomsky, *At War with Asia* (Vintage: 1970), p. 91. Westmoreland's speech was originally reported in the *Christian Science Monitor* (October 27, 1969).

[15] *Ibid.,* pp. 91–92. The full text of Sullivan's remarks is in the *Congressional Record,* August 8, 1969, F9589.

Try it all out in Southeast Asia. See what works.

The point is that technique—and the ultimate in technique lies in modern weapons—is governed by the criterion of efficiency, which becomes the determining factor of every decision. In technique, decisions are made according to means which inexorably become ends. Ends disappear in the reality of technique, overwhelmed by means. Techniques are all calculated means—rational, efficient means which obscure quickly all goals and become the ends themselves, as the means of modern warfare have repeatedly overwhelmed all political ends. For example, according to an Assistant Secretary of Defense, the decision to bomb North Vietnam "was taken, at least in part, because it was one of the things that the United States military forces were best prepared to do."[16] The technique was "our best," the most efficient available, given the nature of the Pentagon machine over against Vietnamese peasants (and given the restraining power of world opinion against use of the ultimate means, nuclear weapons). As the most efficient technique, it had to be tried—and if eventually modified or abandoned from lack of results, then abandoned from no loss of faith in technique (which would have compelled conversion to a more human criterion), but abandoned in favor of a new, more efficient technique: Shift the bombing to Laos and Cambodia.

The primary value and spiritual key of the technological society is efficiency—what works, according to a purely pragmatic gauge of effectiveness. *How to* sell the product; get the grade; beat the market; win the election; control public opinion; win the minds and hearts of an

[16] Adam Yarmolinsky, Principal Deputy Assistant Secretary of Defense for International Security Affairs, 1965–66. Quoted by Chomsky, p. 85.

Asian people; kill them efficiently if they can't be won. How to determine and master the technique so as to get results. How to be not wise or human, but effective— how to choose the one best means, which will become its own end until a more efficient means is found. We choose—because we must—whatever is effective. The most efficient technique chooses us.

The question at issue is, in the symbolic terms we began with from Huxley's *Island:* What is the relation between *moksha*-medicine and motor scooters (which Huxley regarded as opposites)? Or the same question set in an understanding of the technological society: What is the relation between psychedelic contemplation and technique? And to put it a third way, adding another dimension: What effect has technique had upon the historical development of the contemplative life up to the appearance of psychedelics?

Thomas Merton took up the question in this third form, in some notes he wrote during the final year of his life which provide an important critical insight on psychedelic contemplation. He reflected on something that to his knowledge had never been studied, the influence of science and scientific method on the monastic mentality and on the monastic concept of discipline:

Anyone who is acquainted with early monastic and patristic literature is aware that for the Fathers discipline and ascesis were not simply sure-fire methods which paid off in results provided you followed all the instructions and carried out all the proper steps in the right order. This concept of discipline in the life of prayer did however arise in the fifteenth and sixteenth centuries, about the same time as the concept of scientific method developed (Bacon, Descartes). It quite evidently influenced the Jesuits—perhaps not so much

Ignatius himself who was more subtle and more experienced, but doubtless the Ignatian school. *The idea
was that if you set up the right conditions, a kind of
laboratory of prayer, and if you carried out the experiment according to instructions, you would get the
desired result. You could work things out so that you
obtained the precise kind of grace you were looking
for. This concept has by now evolved into the simple
pharmacology of contemplation: you take the right pill
and you turn on. Hence the idea of discipline was
corrupted into a kind of methodology,* and, as in the
case of social sciences for instance (where the same kind
of transposition took place), instead of really praying
and meditating, people became obsessed with their
"method" and observed themselves at prayer, checking
on the method and wondering why they were not getting
the desired results. Without going further into this important question, it has to be said here and now that this
transformation of a discipline in a broad, human measure and in a theological climate of love and grace into
a methodology of will and concentration has been fatal
to Catholic contemplation.[17]   (emphasis added)

The question of psychedelic contemplation has to do
with the progressive corruption of prayer into a methodology or technique. Contemplative prayer became a
technique when, under the influence of the scientific
method, spiritual writers began to emphasize the means
of prayer which if followed properly would result in
stages of the spiritual life. One then went through a certain order of spiritual exercises so as to arrive at God. The
hardly noticed shift in the contemplative life which had
thus taken place was, from the Desert Fathers' teaching, of asceticism as a means of reining in the self and
becoming open to the unpredictable movements of the

---

[17] Thomas Merton, "Renewal and Discipline in the Monastic Life"
(*Cistercian Studies:* Vol. V, 1970: 1), pp. 6–7.

Spirit, to a spiritual technique which if followed correctly would result in a pre-designated kind of experience. Whereas the Desert Father had gone into the wilderness to open himself to the terrible power of the Unknown, the modern contemplative went into the monastery to follow a method of prayer and asceticism believed to be the most efficient means, "the one best way," to reach God. The contrast is, as Merton puts it, between "forcing the issue and getting what you want" (through the most effective means) and "learning the ways of the spirit and of grace, being ready and open to respond to the unpredictable working of a God whose ways are 'not our ways.'"[18]

In the light of this analysis, we can begin to see why psychedelics may not be the ramparts against motor scooters, or the environment of technique, which Aldous Huxley presented them as being. If we see psychedelics within the history of the methodology of technique and its growing control over all contemporary attitudes and actions, from bombing raids to spiritual exercises, then psychedelics seem something less than "a frontal assault" on the technological society. On the contrary, within this perspective of the technicizing of the spirit, "the pharmacology of contemplation" can in fact be seen as the potential revolutionary's final surrender to the rule of the technological society.

Technique claims absolute efficiency in every field of human activity, and psychedelics claim that efficiency in achieving the mystical experience. There need be nothing irrational or unpredictable about the visitation of the Holy upon the inner life of man. As Allan Cohen said as a critic of psychedelics, and as proponents of the LSD

[18] *Ibid.*, p. 7.

experience have insisted from the beginning, "If I stick
you in a church and give you 500 micrograms of LSD
I will guarantee you a religious experience." Psychedelics
represent the ultimate in efficiency, the technicizing of
1. (God.) In the psychedelic experience of divinity, I control the experience of God by pulling the lever of technique—by dropping the pill. To drop or not to drop:
That is the question of my mystical experience. The encounter with God is available through my local drug
dealer.

Psychedelics, *moksha* or "liberation" medicine, are the
technological society's final denial of liberation's possibility by submitting the contemplative—who in the desert of the Spirit had been the most transcendentally
free man of his time, hence the most threatening and
most liberating to society—to the reign of technique
which is the spiritual form of man's enslavement today.
In the environment of technique, technique chooses the
contemplative's way as it does all others. Given the goal
of mystical experience and the criterion or efficiency, the
scientized methodology of the monastery of the ascesis
of the East can only be replaced by the more effective
technique of swallowing the right pill. It is the "one
best way," or as Doctor McPhail says of *moksha*-medicine,
"the easy way." Why choose a less effective way, unless
one is plagued by "the puritan's sense of guilt in en-
joying anything for which he has not suffered" or "embarrassment at the fact that anything genuinely spiritual
can come out of a bottle" (as Alan Watts says in char-
acterizing resistance to psychedelics)?[19] Psychedelics are
the way because psychedelics work.

[19] Watts, pp. 19, 20.

But as Aldous Huxley acknowledges by the conclusion of *Island*, however much psychedelics may work internally and even socially to the point of dampening immediate desires for motor scooters, they provide no ground for resistance to the ultimate means of the technological society, tanks and guns. Psychedelics belong to a way of life which in the last analysis encourages the establishment of a totalitarian state. In the novel's conclusion, as the journalist Will Farnaby now finally converted to the ways of Pala is undergoing his first reality-revelation through *moksha*-medicine, he witnesses the reality of Murugan's sudden takeover of Pala. Murugan leads a small convoy of armored cars up a main street and assumes complete control of the island on behalf of the dictator of a nearby state, Colonel Dipa, by firing a burst of shots into Dr. McPhail. As the armored cars go back down the night street, their headlamps light up briefly the serenely smiling face of the great stone Buddha: "Disregarded in the darkness, the fact of enlightenment remained."[20]

But enlightenment can be given no public testimony from the ground of psychedelic contemplation. Huxley has already made clear in a previous passage how inconceivable any public resistance to a dictatorship would be to a people whose freedom has been won by *moksha*-medicine. In response to Will Farnaby's question, "And what will you do if the worst happens?" (meaning Murugan's takeover on behalf of Colonel Dipa), a young woman who represents the best of Pala replies:

> "Try to make the best of it, I suppose. Even in the worst society an individual retains a little freedom. One

[20] *Island*, p. 295.

perceives in private, one remembers and imagines in private, one loves in private, and one dies in private—even under Colonel Dipa."[21]

She then suggests that Farnaby have some *moksha*-medicine.

If one perceives, loves, and dies in private, without protest and resistance to murder, then the public dimension is given over without contest to the rule of the technicians, and without dissent to everything their rule implies for the people not only of a single island—for there is no isolated paradise left—but of the entire earth. Once *moksha*-medicine has absorbed contemplation into technique, resistance to oppression is dead, because the contemplative—the potential satyagrahi-resister—has become a creature of the technological society. The contemplative has thus lost the ground for his resistance. For the power to resist is dependent on the square of earth on which the Buddha sits independent of his society, liberated from the world's slavery by his enlightenment; or dependent on the rock of faith outside the world which Thomas Merton believed the contemplative had to stand upon, in order to pull drowning men from the swift-flowing current of their society's madness. Resistance is dependent on contemplation, not a counterfeit contemplation of technique in which the contemplative uses a form of the oppression to guarantee "a religious experience," but a contemplation transcending the technological mind-set of modern man and exposing the person of faith to the chilling, liberating demands of a Spirit which blows like a hurricane where it will.

What remains finally, when psychedelics have confined the contemplative to the dimensions of technique,

21 *Ibid.*, p. 270.

is, as Huxley shows truly in his novel, the totalitarian reality without public opposition. *Island* reveals the inevitable victory of technique, even as Huxley sought to avoid it by recommending means which take part in it. That Huxley became a leading exponent of liberation through psychedelics in the final years of his life, and had hopes for a Pala that would endure, was an ironic outcome for the author of *Brave New World*, which had been written partly as a warning against the possibility (or probability) of oligarchical governments using barbiturates, hypnosis, and psychological suggestion to enslave "even the most recalcitrant subjects," as Huxley once wrote to George Orwell.[22]

The social basis for Huxley's argument for psychedelics, as exemplified by an essay written late in his life, was his sense of planetary haste:

> In a world of explosive population increase, of headlong technological advance and of militant nationalism, the time at our disposal is strictly limited. We must discover, and discover very soon, new energy sources for overcoming our society's psychological inertia, better solvents for liquefying the sludgy stickiness of an anachronistic state of mind.[23]

Thus Huxley felt compelled to include in his recommendations for a quickly redeemed humanity "a course of chemically triggered conversion experiences or ecstasies," "through the use of harmless psychedelics."[24] But as Jacques Ellul has pointed out in *The Technological Society*, haste is also one of the foremost characteristics

[22] This point is made by Stephen Spender in his review-article, "The Conscience of the Huxleys" (*The New York Review of Books*: March 25, 1971), p. 22.

[23] Aldous Huxley, "Culture and the Individual," in *LSD: The Consciousness-Expanding Drug*, p. 47.

[24] *Loc. cit.*

of technique. It is haste to which efficiency responds and then expresses. We are back to an argument of efficiency, because mankind can't wait. But liberation from technique lies deeper than technical solutions, seized upon in this case partly from the compassion of a great man who felt humanity's crisis and partly from the impulse of haste which was a defining characteristic of the social slavery he struggled to overcome.

Whereas Huxley's *Island* presents the case for psychedelics in terms of a utopian society created largely through their use, Alan Watts' *Joyous Cosmology* describes the experience of a single man in his experiments with psychedelics. *The Joyous Cosmology* follows a psychedelic genre begun by Huxley in his book, *The Doors of Perception,* which was his autobiographical account of the effects on his consciousness of his first use of mescaline. Although Watts in writing a similar work disclaims any "hope to surpass Aldous Huxley as a master of English prose," he believes with Leary and Alpert that he is pushing beyond Huxley, who himself "by now [1962], through subsequent experiments, knows that [psychedelics] can lead to far deeper insights than his book described." Thus, says Watts:

> I feel that the time is ripe for an account of some of the deeper, or higher, levels of insight that can be reached through these consciousness-changing "drugs" when accompanied with sustained philosophical reflection by a person who is in search, not of kicks, but of understanding.[25]

[25] Watts, p. xvii. Another important book, which makes no argument for hallucinogenic drugs but which in the counter-culture has influenced their use, is *The Teachings of Don Juan: A Yaqui Way of Knowledge* by Carlos Castaneda (Ballantine Books: 1969). *The Teachings of Don Juan* is a fascinating account of the four-year apprenticeship of Castaneda, a graduate student in anthropology at UCLA, under Don Juan, an old

Huxley's final book, *Island,* and Watts' *Joyous Cosmology* together comprise the two major elements in a theology of psychedelics. In Huxley's and Watts' proclamation of the psychedelic good news, *Island* is the eschatological vision, the final communal form of the kingdom of God, and *The Joyous Cosmology* is its incarnational form, the kingdom as realized within a single believer now. As the foremost statement of psychedelic contemplation from within, *The Joyous Cosmology* can serve us here as a second, more interior measure of the liberating power of psychedelics.

The Joyous Cosmology is a synthesis of several drug experiences, written as if the whole occurred on one day in a single place. Much of it is a description of Watts' transformed impression of the natural world, described in language which vibrates with the tones and feeling of life. There can be little question in one's mind, after traveling the pages of Watts' *Joyous Cosmology,* that psychedelics are capable of heightening one's sensitivity to the cosmos, seen through Watts' eyes radiating outward with exquisite detail from a bursting bud in the garden, "whose depth of light and structure go on forever," to the evening sunset which "closes a day that seemed to have been going on since the world began."[26]

Yaqui Indian, after Castaneda has urged Don Juan to teach him "about peyote." Castaneda then goes through hundreds of hours of instruction under Don Juan and fourteen "sessions" with three different natural hallucinogens. In the course of the instruction, Don Juan makes clear that his way of knowledge is not about peyote as Castaneda understands it but is rather a disciplined and sometimes terrifying exploration of the unconscious. The problem of the book is that Castaneda never does understand that Don Juan is a guru of the unconscious, although as a student he is a careful reporter of the old Indian's teaching. In a drug culture the book is easily misread as having more to do with hallucinogens than with an acceptance of the unconscious.

26 Watts, pp. 27, 76.

Watts shows in detail how psychedelics can intensify one's perception of the physical world.

He also claims that through psychedelic contemplation, as in other mystical experiences, the individual becomes

> so peculiarly open and sensitive to organic reality that the ego begins to be seen for the transparent abstraction that it is. In its place there arises (especially in the latter phases of the drug experience) a strong sensation of oneness with others, presumably akin to the sensitivity which enables a flock of birds to twist and turn as one body. A sensation of this kind would seem to provide a far better basis for social love and order than the fiction of the separate will.[27]

This insight does seem to lay the basis for some kind of social dynamic through the psychedelic state. As Watts says in his conclusion, psychedelics may help in the evolution of a new image of man "as an organism inseparable from his social and natural environment." Psychedelic contemplation, by temporarily dissolving our defenses, permits us to see "what separative consciousness normally ignores—the world as an interrelated whole." This vision bears "a striking resemblance to the unfamiliar universe that physicists and biologists are trying to describe here and now."[28]

As is evident from Watts' language in elaborating the psychedelic sensation of oneness with others, both in his retrospective conclusion and in the course of describing his experience, the others who happen to be people pass easily into a cosmic scene. The joyous cosmology is a dancing universe in which distinct persons are an illusion. There is a reason for this: The ego which is so

[27] *Ibid.*, p. 90.
[28] *Ibid.*, p. 94.

"transparently abstract" in Watts is equally transparent in his perception of others, so much so that the physical universe becomes an easily convertible reality with the persons who happen to be standing in the forefront of one's environment. "Unfortunately our forms of speech follow the design of the social fiction which separates the conscious will from the rest of the organism, making it the independent agent which causes and regulates our actions."[29]

The significance of this perception becomes evident in the climactic passage of *The Joyous Cosmology,* at a point in Watts' psychedelic experience when he feels his understanding "dawning into a colossal clarity, as if everything were opening up down to the roots of my being and of time and space themselves," and he is compelled to reveal what he understands. Watts' revelation and his commentary on it deserve to be quoted in full:

> The sense of the world becomes totally obvious. I am struck with amazement that I or anyone could have thought life a problem or being a mystery. I call to everyone to gather round.
>
> "Listen, there's something I *must* tell. I've never, never seen it so clearly. But it doesn't matter a bit if you don't understand, because each one of you is quite perfect as you are, even if you don't know it. Life is basically a gesture, but no one, no thing, is *making* it. There is no necessity for it to happen, and none for it to go on happening. For it isn't being driven by anything; it just happens freely of itself. It's a gesture of motion, of sound, of color, and just as no one is making it, it isn't *happening* to anyone. There is simply no problem of life; it is completely purposeless play—exuberance which is its own end. Basically there is the gesture. Time, space,

[29] *Ibid.*, p. 89.

and multiplicity are complications of it. There is no reason whatever to explain it, for explanations are just another form of complexity, a new manifestation of life on top of life, of gestures gesturing. Pain and suffering are simply extreme forms of play, and there isn't anything in the whole universe to be afraid of because it doesn't happen to anyone! There isn't any substantial ego at all. The ego is a kind of flip, a knowing of knowing, a fearing of fearing. It's a curlicue, an extra jazz to experience, a sort of double-take or reverberation, a dithering of consciousness which is the same as anxiety."

Of course, to say that life is *just* a gesture, an action without agent, recipient, or purpose, sounds much more empty and futile than joyous. But to me it seems that an ego, a substantial entity to which experience happens, is more of a minus than a plus. It is an estrangement from experience, a lack of participation. And in this moment I feel absolutely *with* the world, free of that chronic resistance to experience which blocks the free flowing of life and makes us move like muscle-bound dancers. But I don't have to overcome resistance. I see that resistance, ego, is just an extra vortex in the stream— part of it—and that in fact there is no actual resistance at all. There is no point from which to confront life, or stand against it.[30]   (Watts' emphasis)

This is a remarkable passage, both in its sharp sense of a climactic insight ("Eureka! . . .") and in the nature of the insight granted by the psychedelic experience at its highest point to a philosopher "in search, not of kicks, but of understanding."

Watts' psychedelic insight is that life is basically a gesture, a gesture made by no one. Life is without purpose, and history without responsible agents. Neither God nor man acts in history, and the action of life is

[30] *Ibid.*, pp. 70–73.

without doer and receiver: "just as no one is making it, it isn't *happening* to anyone." Life, then, can be crystallized in our understanding as "completely purposeless play—exuberance which is its own end."

The conclusion is the solution of the problem of pain and suffering. They, too, are "simply extreme forms of play, and there isn't anything in the whole universe to be afraid of because it doesn't happen to anyone!" Thus one is free to "feel absolutely *with* the world." The world and a free-flowing life are one, and any resistance to the world or life derives from an illusionary ego: "There is no point from which to confront life, or stand against it."

Alan Watts reached this insight into the meaning of life and the world in an experience of psychedelic contemplation whose primary setting, he says in his prologue, was "a country estate on the West Coast with garden, orchard, barns, and surrounding mountains."[31] It deserves respect within that setting. It also deserves comparison with non-psychedelic insights reached in other settings, for example, the view of life found in the diary of a street scavenger, Carolina Maria de Jesus, written in her shack in the midst of a *favela* in São Paulo, Brazil:

> I classify São Paulo this way: The Governor's Palace is the living room. The mayor's office is the dining room and the city is the garden. And the favela is the back yard where they throw the garbage.
>
> It seems that the slaughterhouse threw kerosene on their garbage dump so the *favelados* would not look for meat to eat. I didn't have any breakfast and walked around half dizzy. The daze of hunger is worse than that of alcohol. The daze of alcohol makes us sing, but

[31] *Ibid.*, p. 24.

the one of hunger makes us shake. I know how horrible it is to only have air in the stomach.

I began to have a bitter taste in my mouth. I thought: is there no end to the bitterness of life? I think that when I was born I was marked by fate to go hungry. I filled one sack of paper. When I entered Paulo Guimarães Street, a woman gave me some newspapers. They were clean and I went to the junk yard picking up everything that I found. Steel, tin, coal, everything serves the *favelado*. Leon weighed the paper and I got six cruzeiros.

I wanted to save the money to buy beans but I couldn't because my stomach was screaming and torturing me.

I decided to do something about it and bought a bread roll. What a surprising effect food has on our organisms. Before I ate, I saw the sky, the trees, and the birds all yellow, but after I ate, everything was normal to my eyes.

It finally stopped raining. The clouds glided toward the horizon. Only the cold attacked us. Many people in the favela don't have warm clothing. When one has shoes he won't have a coat. I choke up watching the children walk in the mud. It seems that some new people have arrived in the favela. They are ragged with undernourished faces. They improvised a shack. It hurts me to see so much pain, reserved for the working class. I stared at my new companion in misfortune. She looked at the favela with its mud and sickly children. It was the saddest look I'd ever seen. Perhaps she has no more illusions. She had given her life over to misery.

There will be those who reading what I write will say—this is untrue. But misery is real.

What I revolt against is the greed of men who squeeze other men as if they were squeezing oranges.[32]

---

[32] *Child of the Dark: The Diary of Carolina Maria de Jesus,* translated from the Portuguese by David St. Clair (Signet: 1962), pp. 34–35, 45, 47.

The reasons for juxtaposing the reflections of a psychedelic philosopher at the height of his experience, and a
street scavenger in her daily struggle with misery, are:
(1) Their views of life conflict sharply. The philosopher has solved the problem of pain through a psychedelic experience of life as play; the scavenger looks about
her and observes that misery is real. The philosopher
says resistance to the world is illusory and egocentric;
the scavenger revolts against the world in order to survive. (2) At this point in history (perhaps at any time
but especially now), the *favela* setting of Carolina Maria
de Jesus is much more representative of humanity's condition than is Alan Watts' country estate. (3) It is doubt-
ful if the *favela* setting which represents the more common human condition would be conducive to anyone's
good trip, even if psychedelics were available to slum-
dwellers or if high philosophers were transported to gar-
bage-dump shacks. (4) Contemplation, as Watts says, involves a profound experience of oneness with others.
But if the realization of that oneness demands that all
men be gathered together on a country estate, while
turned-on philosophers lead them in play, then we are
far from having realized the condition for psychedelic
truth and unity. In the meantime, as Carolina Maria de
Jesus says, "misery is real." And misery demands of
the contemplative attention, a recognition of men's responsibility for that misery, and resistance to its sources,
if oneness is to have any existential meaning.

Alan Watts is certainly right that Western middle-class
man, enslaved by the mind-set of technique, needs to
rediscover the value of play. But even apart from the
question of achieving this through psychedelic techniques, such a man needs to rediscover play in the con-

text of the global misery for which he is largely responsible. The two attitudes, of play and a deep recognition of human responsibility for change, are not incompatible. Anyone who has had the simple experience of seeing a film clip of Mohandas Gandhi bantering with his British oppressors, or who has had the privilege of witnessing Cesar Chavez shouting encouragement on a picket line or Dan and Phil Berrigan smiling in handcuffs, knows that the strongest resistance to oppression is animated by a profound joy. The act of resistance in men such as these is the yang side of a contemplative joy and awareness that love and truth are real, that when lived to their fullest they are the deepest forces in life, and that a man joined to their power is an embodiment of God's transforming power in history.

Mohandas Gandhi also believed that ego was more of a minus than a plus. But in his never-ending struggle to reduce his ego to zero so as to achieve pure union and liberation, Gandhi realized the end in the process, not as a life which is just a gesture while people suffer and die but as a life of unrelenting and joyful service to all that lives. In that contemplative realization, that liberation demands self-surrender which then issues in service, Gandhi discovered the way of liberation which is the play of the satyagrahi:

> God demands nothing less than complete self-surrender as the price for the only real freedom that is worth having. And when a man thus loses himself, he immediately finds himself in the service of all that lives. It becomes his delight and his recreation. He is a new man never weary of spending himself in the service of God's creation.[33]

[33] M. K. Gandhi, *Hindu Dharma* (Ahmedabad, Navajivan Publishing House: 1950), p. 109.

It has been said by the counter-culture that "the drug revolution" is really all about the fact that many middle-class young people cannot stand being in a social mansion surrounded by a global ghetto. Thus they bomb themselves with drugs, corrode their egos with acids. As a revolutionary step, this still leaves something to be desired—namely, the transformation of the global ghetto around them—and it is not yet evident how psychedelic drugs have aided in that task. The psychedelic visions of Aldous Huxley's utopian island and Alan Watts' joyous cosmology on a country estate appear in the last analysis as further illusions in the mansion of technique unlikely to generate any transforming response to the ghetto beyond. Yet in the age of the global ghetto, a sustained resistance to mass exploitation and killing is the outward expression, the validating fruit, of a genuine inner liberation. To translate Jesus into the moment: By their resistance you shall know them.

At least one psychedelic contemplative has claimed that the LSD experience leads inevitably to resistance, but a resistance of questionable liberation. The original psychedelic prophet, Timothy Leary, has come to equate the inner bombing of the ego with an outer blast of dynamite. As he told an interviewer from his exile in Algiers, after he had broken out of a California jail with the help of Weathermen ("also on acid"):

> Anyone who's been through the whole LSD experience with us is an acid revolutionary now. Dynamite [TNT dynamite] is just the white light, the flash, the external manifestation of the inner white light of the Buddha.[34]

[34] Quoted by Bob Greenfield, "Tim Leary: or, Bomb for Buddha" (*Rolling Stone:* December 2, 1970), p. 20.

But if this is the yin-yang of contemplation and resistance, a vindictive yang seems suddenly to have gained
the upper hand, even as a self-revolving yin was Leary's
contemplative interpretation of the psychedelic Buddha.

Resistance and contemplation unite in the satyagrahi
revolutionary as a single, harmonious way of liberation.
Thus, as Gandhi taught, the measure of all resistance is
a contemplation sunk in the depths of human suffering:

> Recall the face of the poorest and the most helpless
> man whom you have seen and ask yourself if the step
> you contemplate is going to be of any use to him.
> Will he be able to gain anything by it? Will it restore
> him to control over his own life and destiny?[35]

And contemplation in order to form and sustain resistance must be, as the *Bhagavad-Gita* taught Gandhi,
a dark night of inner renunciation liberating the soul
into a light deeper than any perception: "What is night
for all beings is the time of waking for the disciplined
soul."[36]

[35] These words of Gandhi are in large letters at the shrine-area of his
cremation-place at Rajghat. They are quoted by Eileen Egan in "Crossing
India" (*The Catholic Worker*: February 1971), p. 7.

[36] *Bhagavad-gita*, in *A Sourcebook in Indian Philosophy*, edited by Sarvepalli Radhakrishnan and Charles A. Moore (Princeton University
Press: 1957), p. 112.

A critique of psychedelic contemplation arrives at the conclusion that contemplation without resistance to the to-
talitarianism of technique, and to an unjust social order,
is a form of spiritual sterility. Psychedelics are only one
example of popular ways to liberate the spirit which are
finally recognizable as counterfeits by their lack of resistance to a milieu of technique and exploitation. "Hare
Krishna" is a beautiful dance of life back into the schiz-
ophrenia of suburbia when other people lie dying and
unnoticed across the street (or society) from the chant-
ing. Rock music freaks contemplate through stereo and
submit to exploitation by performers who sing as rebels
and live as mandarins. Contemplation without resistance
to an exploitative milieu (in which the counter-culture
often functions as microcosm) is not freedom but capitulation.

But what of the pole opposite psychedelic contemplation, the pole of activist struggle and militant resistance?
Is there a corresponding danger there of reducing the way
of liberation to the yang of its purely social dimension?

The Winter of 1970–71 was for the radical movement
in America a winter of suicides and bombings. Julius

Lester, a black revolutionary and writer whose "Aquarian Notebook" in the pages of *Liberation* served as one of the most sensitive gauges of that time, saw an indictment of the radical movement in the suicide of one revolutionary he knew.

Bob Starobin was a white teacher and scholar in black history. He was a post-doctoral fellow for the Society for the Humanities at Cornell University and had been active in the radical movement there. Several months before he killed himself, he had written to Julius Lester:

> I have been struggling all year, especially this summer, with the contradiction between my scholarly interests and profession and my desire to do more revolutionary deeds. The biggest hangup is, of course, the question of terrorism, for though I am armed to the teeth, I still can't figure out under what circumstances to use them, and I still am afraid of violence and death, though I guess this is related to my white privileges, my class background, and my loved ones.[1]

Lester sought a reason for the suicide of such a man, a scholar who wished "to do more revolutionary deeds," and he found it in his politics:

> It is a politics which has no place in it for a quiet scholar like Bob Starobin. It is a politics which regards violent rhetoric and military action as the *sine qua non* of revolution . . . The revolutionary politics of our time made him feel that without a gun, he couldn't be a revolutionary.
>
> Revolutionary politics should have within it the nourishment and comfort necessary to sustain us when we enter the inevitable dark nights of the soul. And the fact that these politics could not sustain Bob Starobin is the most serious indictment possible of those politics.

[1] Julius Lester, "On the Suicide of a Revolutionary," *Liberation* (Spring 1971), p. 65.

At about the same time as Julius Lester was told of Bob Starobin's suicide, I also received news of the self-inflicted death of a friend whose life had been his work in the movement. Lester's analysis is equally applicable to my friend's death: "The revolutionary politics of our time made him feel that without a gun, he couldn't be a revolutionary." So like Bob Starobin he used that gun on the one clear target he could find, which was himself.

The suicides of revolutionaries have corresponded to the sporadic bombings of American banks and courthouses, which are a less internalized expression of the same politics "which regards violent rhetoric and military action as the *sine qua non* of revolution." It seems likely that in a time of increasing governmental repression such a politics of radical reaction will take an increasing toll inward, in the lives of dedicated young people trapped in a political and psychic corner defined by absent executioners. I believe American radicals will continue to be trapped by repression into a suicidal politics until we can discover not so much a new politics as a way of liberation which in the course of political struggle is capable of sustaining us "when we enter the inevitable dark nights of the soul."

In the din of the capitalistic, technological society, which bombs abroad and consumes at home, the basis for a way of liberation can be found in solitude. In solitude, in the depths of a man's own aloneness, lie the resources for resistance to injustice. Resistance arises first from a perception of man's suffering and from the assumption of one's own responsibility to seek the transformation of a murderous system into a human society.

The resister recognizes injustice and inhumanity for what they are and concludes, "I am responsible for either condoning their existence or struggling for change." But for a man to take responsibility in public for his society, he must have the deeper integrity to take responsibility in solitude for his own inner life. Otherwise the only basis for social change will be personal alienation, and one's act of resistance will be less a response to injustice than a flight from solitude. For it is in solitude that the most fearful encounter of all confrontation politics must take place: facing the emptiness of my self.

The truth which comes home in solitude is that *I* am powerless to change the world of man's suffering. The truth which comes home in solitude is that no movement, no organization, no strategy, no individual, and most certain of all, no power in *me*, is capable of transforming the world as it kills and dies into that ultimate vision which Marx described as a classless society and Jesus through John as a new heaven and a new earth. The truth which comes home in solitude is that the struggle for liberation must begin by recognizing the terrifying emptiness and impotence of that self of mine which is so prepared to pose on the outside as a redeemer of others. The truth which comes home in solitude is that the "I" who resists, who refuses to live in fear of the state's punishment, is in reality chained to the cell of its own fears and self-fantasies. The truth which comes home in solitude is that I the resister and revolutionary am not God, and that what I *am* therefore falls infinitely short of the power to realize the vision which the revolution proclaims as goal. The truth which comes home in solitude is that the revolution for a new humanity is worth loving for, struggling for, dying for, but that measured by me as its representative the revolution hasn't begun—humanity should look elsewhere for its redemption. The truth which comes home in solitude is that beneath the movement, beneath the solidarity of brotherhood and sisterhood, beneath the redemptive community as currently identified and experienced— the truth which comes home in solitude is that beneath all these new families of man, *I* am alone. And the truth which movement politics shield behind ten thousand slogans for a radicalized world, all men together in freedom, but a truth which solitude cannot hide, is that in fact, now, in reality—I *know* I am alone and unfree. In the clear awareness of solitude I am the living refutation of the revolutionary's dream.

Solitude is my home but I flee from it. I am not prepared to deal with its truth. Few men are. And the great temptation of resistance is that I will resist to avoid dealing with the truth of solitude. But if I do, my resistance will become an evasive struggle with external power, the struggle to refuse others' power and eventually to overpower and govern them. My resistance will become an egotistic duel with external powers because I have not come to terms with the fundamental question of power, power's absence in myself.

This is not a question of whether or not I am able to resist, or whether or not I should. In the age of genocide to be human is to resist. The possibility of resisting is inherent in my consciousness of being a man who chooses in a world of unjustly suffering millions. I can and should choose life, the life of all men, which is bound up in my choice to resist their destruction.

But though I must choose life to be human, who is this "I" who so chooses? I who choose to resist am in my self powerless to overcome the system's evil because that evil is somehow bound up in my very recognition of its existence. And the intensity of my recognition of evil, necessary to my resistance and my humanity, heightens the consciousness of my self which is the source of my powerlessness. I resist, therefore I am: powerless to *be* a liberating force. The power of liberation is beyond me—finally, when I see it more clearly, it is beneath me—in that which fully is without division from its source. But *I* am alone. In resisting the system I resist out of my own powerlessness, and my sense of powerlessness deepens with my commitment of resistance.

I in my commitment cannot end the war, nor can *we*, nor can hundreds of thousands of us marching together, nor millions merely registering our opinions. We *could* perhaps end the war and transform our society as well through massive non-violent civil disobedience, millions of Americans uniting conviction and action and overflowing courtrooms and prisons so that an Asian people might live, but the realization of such a vision would assume a conversion process in American society which is infinitely beyond the power to effect it of any "us" I know. The vision of Americans young and old, hip and straight, joining to live out a massively militant non-violent creed as Gandhi's India did, thus stripping power from the Pentagon and the corporations, is a dream like Martin Luther King's dream in Washington. For its realization we need many Martin Kings, which is to say we need a power of liberation moving in our midst. In the meantime, the question is always, "What do we do now?" No matter what we do: The war, other wars, global exploitation and murder, go on. But we *must* do something because in the midst of the killing our resistance remains the possibility of other men's lives, and our solidarity with them remains the very basis of our own humanity. But what do we *do* now? How can *we* make this war end, make this society and this world more human? The house is burning, there are children inside. Brothers and sisters, we have to get those children out now!

All men are human in their pain and their radical poverty. All men fail to deal with their own powerlessness, fail to live at the center of an undivided power of liberation. Those with the courage to see most sharply the burning house, with the courage to hear most profoundly the cries of the children, are liable to fail most dramatically in the eyes of the world in dealing with their own powerlessness. For the world's resolution of the tension between conscience and society is to demand all for an unjust society, in exchange for which the individual is granted a modicum of personal security to mask his impotence and capitulation. To the world the counter-testimony of the movement, and especially of the lone resister and prophet, is seen as impractical, idealistic, mad. Conscience is society: I am powerless not only because of the *me* who comes home in honest solitude but because of *them* whom I confront every moment and surrender to as my legislators, so that I may then identify with the power of the state. Resistance to them is insanity. The real is social coercion. One acts and reacts wholly within a system of murder. Live and let die.

The reality of my radical powerlessness is covered by the world with the system. It is covered by the movement with the revolution, less securely in this case because here the burning house is acknowledged, and moreover, the meaning of the revolution is the struggle to free those inside: I see the children's faces in the window, and perhaps I even see myself. The prophet is therefore engaged in a double struggle: to respond with all his power to those whose suffering becomes his own, and at the same time to accept his personal and human limits which are based on a radical poverty of being. No man succeeds completely in coming to terms with his poverty of being, and the prophet's struggle is the most intense of all. For the prophet goes to the depths of the double poverty in the world and himself, in the terrible suffering of the innocent and in the radical emptiness of himself. The prophet who is able to endure this double struggle defines all over again the beauty and tragedy of man: the dignity of man's commitment to his limitations. Camus: "Perhaps we cannot prevent this world from being a world in which children are tortured. But we can reduce the number of tortured children. And if you don't help us, who else in the world can help us do this?"[2]

I believe that the suicides of some young revolutionaries, and the desperate bombing attacks of others, can be understood in this context—the prophet's failure to deal first with his own radical powerlessness. It is a failure which comes out of the depths of human struggle, where a generation of young people have been forced to live by a warfare state whose acts of genocide are televised and leave no citizen unaware of the crimes done in his name. The failure of the prophet in this context is the human failure of one consumed by the vision of burning children who then in his response to

[2] Albert Camus, "The Unbeliever and Christians," in *Resistance, Rebellion, and Death* (Modern Library: 1960), p. 55.

their suffering overreaches his limits and his own radical poverty. The failure of the world, on the other hand, is its simple refusal to be human, its failure all along to acknowledge the suffering in the human family and the responsibility which men bear for it.

The truth which comes home in solitude is my poverty of being. But an even deeper truth of solitude, if I can accept and affirm my radical poverty of being, is an opening in silence to the mystery of being itself. It is this opening to being which reveals a way of revolution through solitude. To go deep enough in solitude to know one's radical poverty is to know the way of Camus, the way of man's commitment to truth through his limitations. To go even deeper in solitude to experience the mystery of being, and then to live out of that solitary mystery at the heart of the world while resisting on its surface the executioners of the world, is to know the way of Gandhi, the way of man's liberation by a truth which is one with being itself.

Gandhi defined this way of liberation as "satyagraha," an exact definition because "satya" is the Sanskrit term for truth which is derived from "sat" meaning being, while "agraha" means firmness or force. Gandhi also points out that "satya" implies love. "Satyagraha" is therefore that force of truth and love which is one with being. Satyagraha is the force of being which a man begins to embody in the world as he deepens in the realization of a truth which is all truth. Satyagraha is the truth of being in action. As a revolutionary force, it has no limits except the reluctance of its practitioners to sacrifice themselves wholly to the truth. To reduce oneself completely to zero in the struggle for a universally compassionate truth would be to set off an explosion in the world which

would be as powerful spiritually as the atomic bomb
was materially. The spiritual equivalent of the splitting
of the atom would be the union of man the resister
(man at the center of his history) with that truth which
is being, a union entered by man's deepening in the most
radical poverty possible.

Gandhi's description of the way of satyagraha calls
to mind the early Christians' understanding of Jesus' way
of poverty, a way of complete self-emptying to the point
of accepting death on a cross, at which point Jesus was
exalted as Lord (Paul's Letter to the Philippians 2:6–
11). In the Christian's context, then, the explosive power
of satyagraha would be the exaltation of man by God
realized through man's becoming one with Jesus' complete self-emptying on the cross, thereby becoming one
with being.

The mystery of being which is the untapped power
of a satyagraha revolution, and which lies below a poverty radical enough to accept death on a cross, is the
mystery of unity. Being is one. All men are one. Yet
all men are blind to the reality and power of this
oneness, we see it only darkly as an ideal possibility,
or if as a reality then only in moments of intense illumination which fade into the conditioned separations of
society. But the one mystery of being is below all things
and all men. Below the measurable fragments which
claim exclusive reality in our eyes, below the daylight
self which assumes *I* am in control, below the radical
poverty which itself descends a ladder from dark night
into darker morning, below all images and below all
darkness, in the pit of a spiritual void lies the mystery
of being and its unity. This experiential mystery at the
bottom of created reality is not simply the truth that

being is one but the truth-force that its oneness is infinite power—and the power to reestablish an explosive
awareness of the real, of the One, on each successive
level of existence reascending from the unconscious into
consciousness and finally back into the arena of resistance to corporate murder.

The point of the One's emergence in the world, the
point of psychic and political revolution for mankind,
is the man of radical poverty and utter renunciation
of fruits whom Gandhi called the "satyagrahi," the
single-minded practitioner of truth-force in conflict. The
satyagrahi has learned to rest inwardly at the zero-
point of utter solitude while resisting the powers of the
world. Through the satyagrahi's renunciation of power
along a way of radical poverty the truth-force of the
One can reassert a power which is over no one but
within all. This was the effect of Gandhi's fasting in
the midst of cities being destroyed by civil and religious
war, the effect of death-accepting love: Thousands of
people stopped killing one another in an intensely bitter Hindu-Muslim conflict and joined in demonstrations
of peace because the bonds of oneness were restored
from within through the self-emptying of one who loved
them all. The mystery of being's unity is a truth felt
overwhelmingly through the voluntary suffering of one
who loves.

In a revolution through solitude the One is the many,
the many satyagrahis who fan out into a death-infested
society and reignite the fire of unity, the One re-
kindled in the many beyond who make up the people
and whose power lies in a rediscovery of their unity.
Massive non-violent civil disobedience is the goal, the
committed life and action of ever widening communi-

ties arising from a central intuition of the mystery and power of being, truth-force in action. Thus through the rediscovery and expression of a profound unity are the pillars of oppression knocked away: fragmentation of reality and of the people, and the consequent fear of each individual alienated from being and from the family of man. In a revolution through solitude unity reaches out by reaching up through the inner lives of radical poverty which are the fearless base of a people's reunion and transformation. The many are one, not submerged in a mass movement but rooted in a personal awakening which has passed over into the consciousness of an entire people. Revolution through solitude is the transformation of consciousness experienced by a whole people coming together through the radical self-emptying of its prophets, prophets who are able to endure and disperse a murderous spirit of the time because their roots are in a loving truth of being. Gandhi, Martin Luther King, Cesar Chavez, Dom Hélder Cámara serve as signs of the power and possibility of such a revolution.

In the Spring of '71 in Washington, there were more immediate signs—in the spirit of the Vietnam Veterans and the non-violence of the Mayday participants—that such a revolution could occur in America. But as Dan Berrigan makes clear in *The Dark Night of Resistance*, written during his months underground, to articulate and draw upon the spiritual resources for revolutionary change remains an underground struggle in the radical movement itself, which in many of its values is a microcosm of the secular city of America. Only underground and in solitude, away from the marketplace of establishment and radical politics, is it possible to rediscover the roots of genuine change.

In a revolution through solitude the people are one at the same time as each satyagrahi continues to stand utterly alone in the presence of the One, who grants a revolutionary power of community only through the radical poverty and interior silence of each satyagrahi, each man poor in spirit. In a revolution of truth-force, of the power of being, there is no way up except down, no way to power except through renunciation, no way to union in community except through self-surrender in solitude, no way to being except through nothingness.

The way of man's liberation through solitude, the way of revolutionary change in a world of nuclear-powered governments, is through the infinitely silent power of One in whom one lives only by dying.

Part Two: The Way

There are ways but the Way is uncharted.

Tao Te Ching

Enter by the narrow gate, since the road that leads to perdition is wide and spacious, and many take it; but it is <u>a narrow gate</u> and <u>a hard road</u> that leads to <u>life</u>, and only a few find it.

Matthew 7:13–14

The Power of the Way will come into you when you are empty like a valley or canyon, and therefore receptive to it. You will then be sensitive equally to good and bad as they concern you and will be able to test everything for its worth; in the end you will come to terms with the effortless worth that is located in the distant past . . . in the end you will be like the valley which is the favorite resort of the Way and its Power.

Tao Te Ching

I was playing on the soil beneath a pine. The month was June and the wind scuttled clouds along the valley walls. The clouds swirled into the mountains, threatened black explosions on the rocks. They would send a flood from the sky into our valley that would beat down the weeds in the fields and sweep toward me in a drum of current. I felt a beautifully sinister dread shiver through my five-year-old bones. I could run if I had to. The rain wasn't there yet and I was fast. I could beat my sister running. The wind's song warned me that someone was lost, would be lost, beware of clouds and wind-song. I was wary, kept my head down, intent on ant creatures legging their way through dark roots and pine needles. The ants made frenzied sprints along the roots, missed colliding by last-instant dodges. I tried to peer closer, to see their faces stricken by the black threat which would fill their homes, uproot them into the flood. No faces. Only the legs were afraid.

Finally, most intently, I studied my pinecone seed. A crunched-up mash of wood it was, like a wad of paper ready for the fire. The cone had rough edges. I could crunch it a little in both hands. My pinecone was ready for the ground. I was planting it to make a new tree. Tree, grow a hole through the sky! Through the sky.

I dug a shallow bed for my cone-seed and laid it to rest. Up through the sky. I sifted dirt over the cone, breathing my command—through the sky—into its grave. To grow. I would like to grow. Playing under scurry clouds was fun. Their wings made crying sounds against the cliffs. Scurry fast, clouds. Beat the thunder. You, thunder down the valley, I hear you. Scurry over, clouds, down the river, beat that thunder down the valley. The thunder murmured. It was coming. I could see the rain-sheets far down there shift from bluff to bluff in slanting haze lines. The rain drifted to me, like water on the lake when I peered at fish. The haze lines slid against the mountains and made the valley foggy.

The air was good against my T-shirt. I liked a clean chill. And everything was moving, driving to me. Clouds and wind and thunder, come! My cone-seed is down, planted. Come, cry over it. It will grow, but *make* it grow.

Then Nancy came. She was on the path alongside the weed fields and over the fall to the river. She was skimming. I never saw her skim so. The weeds were shivering in the fields and kept me from seeing her legs. Her hair was in the wind like a tumbleweed and you could hear more wind driving the river below, making it roar louder through the valley, but Nancy, small like candlelight, sailed over the roar. She had fluffy brown hair, and it was softly high, bouncing so against the scurry clouds that I knew a great wonder at all the world's moving. Daddy said the world was round and spun, I knew it so, spinning rain and thunder toward me and my sister skimming. I was small and crouching against the ground, antlike. Everything loomed and shook and spun. I held my palms to the ground and pressed to keep from falling. The world was round and maybe I was on the underside. Maybe it would forget to glue me. Don't whirl me into the clouds, world. Not yet. I want to stay. Just till Nancy comes, please. Then I'll let go (she'll keep me from falling). Then whirl away, world (sister-helper, come).

She was there. I let go, made ready to fly. And, secret of secrets lost now, would have flown had her hand failed to touch my hair.

Hi! Hi! Words bounced on the wind, like her fluff of hair still bobbing proud. She was carrying books. Her skirt was flared in the wind. She looked like the Dutch girl on the kitchen wall. Her face was bright. It was clear like a pool of water and I could see myself, too. In her eyes. She had crinkling eyes that squeezed fun at you. It was funny, her eyes against the leaping clouds and me in her eyes, in the clouds then, where my tree would be. Join me there tree, in Nancy's eyes in the clouds.

"Today was my last day of high school, little brother."

"Last day, Nancy?"

"Yes, now I'll go away to college. To a big, big city with buildings as tall as God."

"Can I come?"

Everything was going by and we were still and together, Nancy and I. I was kneeling and looking to my sister up there, who had sent an angel hand to my head. She was looking through to my soul, which was deeper than my body. An eternity-second ticked and the rain came, darting about us until it formed a gauzy curtain

—and then a miracle—the sun split a cloud and rain-
bowed through our curtain. Drops melted along Nancy's
cheeks and made her look like crying. She lifted her
hand from my head and touched her fingers—the nails
so bitten it hurt to look—to the drops on her cheeks. She
woke from a wonder. We waited to see what would
happen. Her eyes narrowed so she couldn't see my soul
any more. Her cheeks got wetter. She dropped her hand
and grabbed mine.

"I'll race you home," Nancy cried.

We ran, flew away, and I beat her.

Do you remember, Nancy? What did you see in that
moment before the rain? I was in your eyes but much
more than I kept us flying over the wind. Could you
see the college and the big, big city with buildings as
tall as God? Was it all more beautiful than our valley?

I grew some then and found it okay. Nancy went away.

TRIAL

I am on trial. I am an American in the belly of leviathan,
my nation-state which exploits the world. I am on trial
because I have realized the nature of the global situation and now recognize my responsibility to resist corporate murder at its source in the United States of
America. Given the facts of American wealth and power
and their cost elsewhere in unseen lives, I am on trial
before humanity and God, struggling in the belly of
the monster to keep false judges from eclipsing the
Real. I am on trial because I am determined to act in
such a way that my government, which now governs
exclusively for a power elite, will become aware of my
joining other brothers and sisters in resistance to it. I
am on trial because *I know* if I live in fidelity to the
truth of resistance as I have realized it, I shall be subject
to trial by the State—or if not that, then successive trials
by my employer, former friends, community opinion—
trial after trial until the judgment rendered everywhere
has been hung above my life and an unending sentence
imposed.

I have taken my first faltering steps into resistance,
and I am on trial because I am being met by increasing

pressures to turn back—while there is still time. I am on trial therefore because my pre-resistance self is fighting for its life, while the Way forward opens into an abyss. At the edge of that abyss, as in the courtroom, each of us stands trial alone. If I deliver my life into resistance, and as a consequence one day stand before the judge who represents imperial power (whether he be magistrate, employer, or respectable opinion), I shall be utterly alone—as I am now in this moment of truth. My trial then is my trial now, for in facing the question of whether or not to step into the abyss I am struggling with my readiness to speak truth to power when power brings me to judgment.

Abandon yourself to the Spirit, said Jesus: "And when they lead you away to hand you over, do not worry beforehand about what to say; no, say whatever is given to you when the time comes, because it is not you who will be speaking: it will be the Holy Spirit" (Mark 13:11).

When Jesus' own moment came before Pilate, the Spirit is reported to have spoken of the kingdom of truth: "Yes, I am a king. I was born for this, I came into the world for this: to bear witness to the truth; and all who are on the side of truth listen to my voice" (John 18:37).

"Truth?" said the judge, "What is that?" and handed Jesus over to the executioners.

"Truth? What is that?" says every judge to every satyagrahi as he signals to the marshals. You know we have our orders, you as citizen-soldier, I as imperial judge. We have our chain of command. And we have a judicial system dedicated to truth enough, as you know from the State's patience here in listening to you.

But don't try to *bear witness* to the truth at the embarrassment of the court. Consult your lawyer for further details.

What is the truth of my trial? (Which is also yours, friend. We are in the same courtroom, and each of us alone.) What is that kingdom of truth which is my only defense in the Spirit when I am tried—alone before the same judge, still on duty, who washed his hands of Jesus' truth? What truth can be the radical power, the spiritual root, of my resistance when my life is placed on trial before the world? Is my resistance mere rhetoric which will crumble when I stand before the judge's power over my life? Or do I believe in a truth which can overcome the world? (Judge, for that moment you *are* the world.)

Jesus prefaced his remarks to Pilate on the kingdom of truth by distinguishing it from another kind of kingdom: "Mine is not a kingdom of this world; if my kingdom were of this world, my men would have fought to prevent my being surrendered to the Jews. But my kingdom is not of this kind" (John 18:36).

Yes to Pilate's query whether Jesus claims power. But *no* to any claim to the kind of power which Pilate represents. The kingdom of truth is not a kingdom of this world. If it were, Jesus' men would have fought to prevent his being taken. In fact, one disciple did begin such a struggle when the Roman troops seized Jesus but was stopped immediately by Jesus. The kingdom of truth is characterized by its renunciation of violence.

Pilate and his successors are unable to understand what truth is because their lives are given over to a power which rules by violence, therefore by untruth. Truth moves people to action through conviction and belief. A government is true and just only to the extent it is non-violent, that is, only to the extent that it governs through a truth of service acknowledged by the people who thus grant it their power of consent and participation. But the ideal of government through truth is rejected in principle by imperialism, whether it be that of Rome in Palestine or the far more powerful military-economic empire of America across the world today. A militarily backed economy which exploits the mass of humanity and lays waste to the earth for the benefit of a powerful few constitutes the greatest kingdom of untruth the world has known. America rules not by truth but by the most destructive military force ever needed to enforce untruth. That kingdom of violence and untruth is the context in which the judge today leans forward to demand of the resister before him, "What is truth?"

Your Honor, it is first of all a categorical rejection of the murderous reality which this court enforces. Leave those robes of dishonor, this system which places the poor in cages, and you may find that truth has again become a possibility.

But the kingdom of truth, while defining itself in clear contrast to the criminality of judge and courtroom, is in Jesus' case almost as far removed from the force of arguing that contrast as it is from the force of violence. Jesus refused to restate his truth before the high priest who questioned him: "I have spoken openly for all the world to hear; I have always taught in the synagogue and in the Temple where all the Jews meet together: I have said nothing in secret" (John 18:20). Nor does Jesus make any effort to persuade Pilate of the truth whose existence Pilate doubts. The truth which Jesus names as his reason for being before Pilate is evidently a truth which while being tried is not redefined, defended by propositions, or proven in debate. Yet its felt strength is sufficient to drive Jesus' judges to distraction—the high priests, then Herod and Pilate, none of whom feels secure with his prisoner—while the prisoner stands quietly before them.

If I am to realize the kingdom of truth, then, in the course of my own trial, I have first of all the Gospel's indication that the radical truth which I would stand upon resists simple verbal formulation, especially when challenged to prove itself in court. The revolution of the kingdom is based on a truth which cannot be identified with eloquent arguments in my defense.

There are opposite dangers here: the first, to surrender my own witness to the representation of a lawyer (or out of court—a public relations expert) whose arguments in my defense will slip quickly into obeisance to judge and empire so as to free me from the law (or public opinion) at any cost to the truth. An act of resistance, or civil disobedience, as represented by most lawyers becomes a plea for toleration by judge and jury, "for the defendant, a respectable member of the community, is obviously of no real danger to law and order and meant no one to follow his peculiar path of witness." The resister who accepts this form of defense (often before realizing the implications of most legal counsel) can console himself with the thought that his lawyer is at least approaching the truth: At this point the resister has *become* no real danger to "law and order," and it is unlikely that what remains of his witness in court will move anyone to follow.

On the other hand, the resister who plays no legal games and challenges directly the heart of the courtroom fallacy, the judge's illegitimacy to judge, will be held in contempt of court. (In trial by public opinion, to disdain that opinion is considered the ultimate form of contempt to society, bringing down immediate judgment.) Which "contempt" may in fact be in the service of truth. But such a response by the resister takes the form of a heavy judgment on the judge himself, which while true in its perception of corporate crime and individual responsibility may prove false to my own purpose on trial of bearing witness to the truth. The judge's crime is not my truth. The judge must be encountered honestly as human and thus lacking the legitimacy to judge others. But his human fallibility and complicity in death are not my direct concern. They must not divert my attention from the fact that it is *I* who am on trial (I would love to believe that it is the judge instead), in the sense that the truth which will or will not sustain me when my very self is threatened by the court is not a truth which can derive its strength from someone else's (judge's or prosecuting attorney's) lack of integrity. The truth of the resister's trial can only be a truth whose inherent power in himself is such that any indictments in conscience which might result from it, as in judge or prosecutor, would arise spontaneously within them when confronted by the simple, radical truth of the accused. As was Jesus, the resister is called to bear witness to the truth. And all who are on the side of truth will listen to his voice.

I seek a radical truth within, in preparation for my trial. I struggle for its power of illumination and the strength to stand within it. And my struggle for a truth to stand within must carry into the trial itself, for the deepest, most living truth emerges through intense conflict seeking reconciliation. Truth is not a slab of concrete to rest my life upon, but a luminous force in which I stand and which I discover is sparked into more dazzling light by the conflict of challenge and response. The court challenges my life: my resistance, my past conduct, whether or not I am to have a future. And if I stand within this luminous truth, I respond out of my very being—Being responds out of me—Truth responds to trial and judgment, and a deeper truth is born in my life and action.

The analogy which is helpful here is that of the Zen student's interview with his *roshi*, or master, during the secluded Zen training period known as *sesshin*. Intellectual theory and abstractions have no place in the interview with the roshi, whose purpose is to encourage the student to experience *satori*, the ultimate truth of enlightenment. In the sharp exchanges with the roshi, which take place periodically as the student strains toward satori, master prods student with his jabbing questions into a more and more direct, unthinking, and deeply psychic response. The student's meditation throughout the day presses like a hot needle on the question of truth which is his *koan*. Then the student summons energies slumbering within him as he approaches his interview and strives to meet the master's challenge with all his inner power, cresting in sudden waves of strength which promise but do not achieve enlightenment. The roshi presses him harder with his questions, strikes him sharply with his baton, seeking to rouse the student's mind further from unawareness into a lightning-flash realization of its true nature. The truth for which the student struggles with his soul is a living truth, a truth in action which when realized will absorb his entire life.

So must be the truth of my trial, though the judge is no Zen master and would hardly understand the courtroom as a possible door to enlightenment. But the point is that the living truth for which a Zen student must be willing to die, in order to realize satori, becomes an existential possibility for me when the situation itself—my trial, the coercion of the court, the judge's closing all doors to freedom—threatens more and more deeply the core of my self. The driving pressures upon a false selfhood which the Zen student *seeks* for the sake of enlightenment, arise naturally in the course of a political trial (or other form of public judgment) whose State-derived purpose is to throttle into submission the revolutionary truth of the resister. The possibility is, then, of a hidden nature, but a strike at an enormous truth of freedom if the resister sees it in time—the shattering of self, and realization of truth, sought by Zen discipline and given to the resister as a possible fruit of the State's very effort to destroy the truth of his resistance. If this possibility is foreseen by the resister as he initiates his act of civil disobedience, then the later step into his trial will come not as an unfortunate consequence of his commitment but as the anticipated culmination of it in a Zen laboratory of truth: Judge, strike sharply as the roshi would strike, for truth shivers below in my being and seeks liberation into my whole life.

Thus the trial of Gandhi. On March 18, 1922, Gandhi was tried by a British court in Ahmedabad on the charge of sedition. The basis of the charge was three of his more challenging articles in his periodical, *Young India*. Gandhi's articles are worth noting both for their statement of uncompromising resistance to imperialism, in his case British imperialism, and as background for understanding the position he took in his trial.

In the first article, "Tampering with Loyalty," Gandhi defined the goal of non-cooperation as revolution and faced squarely the penalty for it:

> Non-cooperation, though a religious and strictly moral movement, deliberately aims at the overthrow of the Government, and is therefore legally seditious in terms of the Indian Penal Code.
>
> . . . We ask for no quarter; we expect none from the Government. We did not solicit the promise of immunity from prison so long as we remained non-violent. We may not now complain, if we are imprisoned for sedition.

In his second article, "A Puzzle and Its Solution" (the British Viceroy, Lord Reading, had said he was "puzzled" by the sight of Indians seeking arrest), Gandhi developed his theme of non-violent resistance to British imperialism in sharper terms:

> We seek arrest because the so-called freedom is slavery. We are challenging the might of this Government because we consider its activity to be wholly evil. We want to overthrow the Government. We want to compel its submission to the people's will. We desire to show that the Government exists to serve the people, not the people the Government. Free life under the Government has become intolerable, for the price exacted for the retention of freedom is unconscionably great.
>
> If the people are behind the sufferers, the Government must yield or be overthrown. If the people are not with them they have at least the satisfaction of not having sold their freedom. In an armed conflict the more violent is generally the victor. The way of peace and suffering is the quickest method of cultivating public opinion, and therefore when victory is attained it is for what the world regards as Truth.

In the third article, "Shaking the Manes" (the reference is to the British Lion), Gandhi envisioned God's destruction of the empire, prayed for non-violence, and refused any submission to British demands:

> No empire intoxicated with the red wine of power and plunder of weaker races has yet lived long in this world, and this "British Empire", which is based upon organized exploitation of physically weaker races of the earth and upon a continuous exhibition of brute force, cannot live if there is a just God ruling the universe . . . I am aware that I have written strongly about the insolent threat that has come from across the seas, but it is high time that the British people were made to realize that the fight that was commenced in 1920 is a fight to the finish, whether it lasts one month or one year or many months or many years and whether the representatives of Britain re-enact all the indescribable orgies of the [Sepoy] Mutiny days with redoubled force or whether they do not. I shall only hope and pray that God will give India sufficient humility and sufficient strength to remain non-violent to the end. Submission to the insolent challenges that are cabled out on due occasions is now an utter impossibility.

Charged in the Ahmedabad court with promoting disaffection to the British government through these articles, Gandhi cheerfully agreed that he had indeed done that. He pled guilty to all the charges. The Advocate-General who was prosecuting the case then asked the judge that a severe sentence be given Gandhi, in particular for the violence which had erupted in several cities during the non-cooperation campaign (ignoring the fact that Gandhi had suspended the campaign precisely because of this violence). The judge asked Gandhi if he wished to make a statement before being sentenced.

It was then in his statement to the court that Gandhi,

as the Zen student before his roshi, requested that the judge strike. Gandhi, however, took a step beyond even the most dedicated Zen student when he asked that the judge, in possession of a power of imprisonment which no Zen master wields, strike him with *all* of his power.

In his statement, Gandhi first of all agreed with the Advocate-General on both the case of sedition which had been made against him and the charge that he was to blame for violence:

> Thinking over these things deeply, and sleeping over them night after night and examining my heart, I have come to the conclusion that it is impossible for me to dissociate myself from the diabolical crimes of Chauri Chaura or the mad outrages of Bombay.*

He traced the development of his own disaffection with the British Empire, from the position of a staunch loyalist to that of an uncompromising non-cooperator, who now felt it his duty to seek that empire's overthrow. Then, in the starkest possible terms, Gandhi confronted the judge with the truth:

> I am here to invite and submit cheerfully to the highest penalty that can be inflicted upon me for what in law is a deliberate crime and what appears to me to be the highest duty of a citizen. The only course open to you, the Judge, is either to resign your post and thus dissociate yourself from evil, if you feel that the law you are called upon to administer is an evil and that in reality I am innocent; or to inflict on me the severest penalty, if you believe that the system and the law you are assisting to administer are good for the people of this country and that my activity is therefore injurious to the public weal.

* Gandhi's statement to the court, and the articles which were the basis for the charge against him, are all quoted in full in *The Great Trial* with an introduction by Mazharul Haque (Ahmedabad: Navajivan Publishing House, 1965).

Judge, feel the truth of an entire life hurled against your presumption to judge it. Feel the power of satyagraha. But if you cannot acknowledge that truth and save yourself, Judge, then strike. Strike with all your power, for truth strains upward from within like a rising explosive, and will flash through my being when you strike, Judge, with that power of repression which will detonate the revolution within.

The judge sentenced Gandhi to six years in prison. Gandhi served two of them. The British remitted the rest of his sentence when a severe illness of Gandhi's made them fear he would die in prison.

If Gandhi had not been fully prepared for the consequences of his challenge in truth to the judge, had he not been standing within that truth with his very being rather than just rhetorically, he would have destroyed both himself and the non-cooperation campaign. In fact he did stand in that truth with his whole life and was able to draw on its power during his imprisonment. At the conclusion of his trial, he is described as leaving the courtroom with a radiant smile. The judge had struck, and truth had exploded within.

Given the witness of Jesus and Gandhi, who stood without fear before their judges and spoke truth to them, I can begin to understand the truth of my trial as the emerging truth of the kingdom.

On trial I must bear witness to the truth. "I was born for this, I came into the world for this: to bear witness to the truth." So it is with every person who steps into the Way, as Jesus did, and is placed on trial. At his last meal with his followers, Jesus said: "I am the Way, the Truth and the Life. No one can come to the Father except through me" (John 14:6). What's that, Jesus?

What is this "Way" which you do not simply follow but *are*, which is the one way to the Father? (The next day he was tried, scourged, and forced to walk a long way.) How are you one with "the Truth"? ("Truth? What is that?" said the judge, and Jesus in silence shouldered the cross.) What makes your life one with "the Life"? ("It is accomplished," he said, and bowing his head, he gave up his spirit.)

"Yes, I am a king," was his reply to the charge. A kingdom of Truth which is the Way and the Life: resistance to untruth—trial—judgment—and the Way lived out in a still more luminous truth. The Gospels say nothing of Jesus' reaction when he was condemned to die. But I believe that standing in the kingdom of truth he must have smiled.

PRISON

In my trial I am called to bear witness to the truth with my life. Bearing witness to the truth means walking the way of truth: That way leads to prison. For the way of truth is the way of liberation—the liberation of all humanity—and thus the way to prison in the midst of a warfare state and economic empire whose prosperity is built on the enslavement of an unseen world. The risk of prison in America is the condition of my deepest freedom because without that risk of truthful living I am already in a prison of my own making, a prison of fear and of self.

What is there to fear, man?

I fear what they can do to me. It is a fear which runs from my seeing it directly, but a fear which I feel identifying itself with all that I have now and would lose—if my fear should be realized, and they should take it all away.

Take what away?

Everything I have.

Like what, for example?

Well, if you want an inventory: job, home, friends, reputation, a way of life which adds up to a secure existence for my family and myself. I fear much more for my wife and family than I do for myself. I have no right to neglect their needs because of my own feelings of conscience. My first duty is to my wife and family.

Your wife is as capable as you are of resistance. Women and men resist together in Indochina. It is in America that men feel such unique obligations toward women: pots and pans for the American woman, napalm for the Vietnamese. Let your family—wife, husband, and children together—be a family of resistance. Grant them all the dignity of entering the real world, where most families suffer while yours prospers.

And what if they refuse?

Then listen, man:

> I have come to set a man against his father, a daughter against her mother, a daughter-in-law against her mother-in-law. A man's enemies will be those of his own household. Anyone who prefers father or mother to me is not worthy of me. Anyone who prefers son or daughter to me is not worthy of me. Anyone who does not take his cross and follow in my footsteps is not worthy of me. Anyone who finds his life will lose it; anyone who loses his life for my sake will find it.

That's going too far.

Just far enough to speak to your condition.

Jesus Christ, you make a very complex matter sound simple. I want to speak to a theologian instead. Or even a bishop.

You know the theologians and bishops are all asleep at this hour. It *is* simple. Listen again: "Happy those who are persecuted in the cause of right: theirs is the *chosen in faith* kingdom of heaven. Happy are you when people abuse you and persecute you and speak all kinds of calumny against you on my account."

Jesus, what a way to live.

The way—entered by a narrow gate.

I've heard all that.

Then believe it.

Gandhi believed and translated it into the context of his own imperialist state:

> For me solitary confinement in a prison cell without any breach on my part of the code of Non-cooperation or private or public morals will be freedom. For me the whole of India is a prison even as the master's house is to his slave. A slave to be free must continuously rise against his slavery and be locked up in his master's cell for his rebellion. The cell door is the door to freedom.

The cell door is the door to freedom because once I am prepared to walk through that door I have nothing to fear. They—whoever "they" may be, perhaps even human beings like myself—can instill no deep fear in me if I am willing to accept the substance of their threat and travel the Way with whatever consequences it may bring. The cell door is the door to freedom if I can acknowledge its threat as the promise of the kingdom.

Nevertheless I am conscious that once I have passed into that cell my freedom can be no Gospel ideal or revolutionary slogan but can only take the form of an experience realized within me, or if not realized, then acknowledged as an illusion. I know, from the few weeks I have already spent in prison for acts of civil disobedience, that a profound sense of freedom behind bars is possible, precisely as Gandhi describes it, but that the experience is likely to diminish as the time behind bars lengthens. In contemplating prison consequences which may be measured not so much in days and weeks as in months and years, I must confront the reality of prison not as an interlude in a white middle-class existence but as a stage of the Way redefining the nature of my life. Prison is then of such duration and intensity that from within the experience I am forced to come to terms with prison as the context of my very life. How free can the choice of prison (through a deliberate act of civil disobedience or a chosen way of life which invites prosecution by the State) remain for me when the severity and duration of my sentence seem to absorb my very life, and instead of feeling myself passing through the role of prisoner I *become* the State's prisoner? What will my sense of freedom be at that point where my principal identity in terms of the institutions of my society is no longer citizen but prisoner?

The question has no answer because no person can know in advance how much he or she can endure for the sake of truth and still come up singing freedom. I cannot know if my belief is rooted deeply enough to sustain me through the worst. The posing of the question is no more than a prayer—a confession of my ultimate powerlessness. But the prayer can be extended into a meditation, and by exploring the resources to sustain my experience of freedom behind the cell door I can know better how solitary my confinement will be.

I remember the valley I was born into, a valley which introduced me to the Way. The Way was present in the valley as the sun and shadow which filled the valley without ever being exhausted by it. Sun and shadow climbed down and up the rock shale and cliffs, over and under the pine trees, sun and shadow moving across the mountain slopes at the edge of the sky, and as night fell, sun fading out overhead as bright stripes in the blue and shadow looming into darkness below.

The Way was in this silent light and change of the valley which filled my being, poured through it, saying nothing but passing my life through day and night, light and dark changes, like the valley's river rippling over a rainbow of rocks which gleamed and disappeared in the flow of light and shadow. The Way was in the silence of the valley, which if one listened to distinguish, was wind brushing trees, river flowing, a car's tires on the highway, and a dog barking down there. So a thinking kind of listening would note that the valley had many sounds in it, which could be accounted for in different ways, but the Way was that flow of life through the valley which remained silent as it entered my being.

The Way of sun and shadow reached in and touched me at the center, and when I looked closely was all of the valley withdrawing into darkness again. I knew the Way as giving itself in the deepest silence. No one ever referred to it. The name "Way" came later as I realized I was walking in it, though I no longer lived in the valley.

I learned to walk in the Way by letting go of the thinking kind of listening, as one did in the valley, and letting silence enter. Another name for the Way was "Guiding Touch." It was no more than that, a touch at the center, and again if I tried to watch too closely it dissolved and there was only myself watching. But its guidance was real and had to be followed: It meant while walking along a way I had assumed (or been told) was right, that I would stop suddenly one morning with people passing on either side, listen, turn slowly, and with utter certitude walk in the opposite direction. If anyone was near enough to notice, the only explanation to an astonished look or question was simply that I'd lost the Way and it lay not there but here.

Finding the Way was not always that simple, and a struggle with it gave me my first experience of prison. I recall a certain point in my life when I began to define my work by the talents of a friend working alongside me. My friend's talents were far greater than my own and seemed required by the nature of the work itself. At first I struggled to overcome my limitations by increasing the pace and reach of my work, trying to jump across great gaps in my inabilities and understanding. But my sense of my limitations deepened and what little understanding I had became confused. The Way was lost, and my situation became inexplicable. It made no sense to have walked this far with certitude, then to discover that my limitations blocked any further progress. Because I *had* to go forward yet had no possible way to do it. I thrashed as one drowning in deep water and went under, to exist as dead matter for what seemed a very long time. The living, caring universe became a gray room in which I sat listlessly or got up to pace occasionally. Nothing and no one could change the fact that I was inwardly dead. Time moved nowhere. I was in prison, locked into myself.

Yet one day while pacing I glanced up and discovered that the Way had begun to reopen before me. It had been impossible to see it in terms of my own ambitions, which had finally collapsed so completely that when I looked up, the Way had reemerged. By defining the end myself I had destroyed the Way, which led elsewhere. I had forgotten the valley, which realized its life through silence. When the valley's silence sang its way in once more, I felt I would never be so arrogant as to lose it again by self-definition, but I did several times and experienced a still harsher imprisonment.

The Way always moved out beyond calculation and thus demanded faith to walk in it. It made no sense to anyone who wanted to secure his future. It demanded that one give up more and more to continue on it. It opened into a sky-clearing light only after a long walking in darkness. The Way then became one in my understanding with the Way of Jesus of Nazareth whose life spoke in the same silence of sun and shadow as the valley did, and whose death-breaking symbols of cross and open tomb declared that the Way was impossibly demanding and incredibly life-giving. Jesus said with his life, death, and resurrection that the Way, when followed in a hostile world, meant love and faith to the point of revolution. Jesus' life said redeem the times—not with your own strength, for you have none and will be destroyed if you rely on it—but redeem the times by joining with others in a community of faith and resistance to death because the Way of Resurrection demands it. My suffering people, the human family, demands it. Truth and love demand it. Your very being demands it. And if you meet the demand, the Way of the valley will sing its deepest silence, its sharpest beauty, into your being in the life-giving form of a cross.

Jesus' Way led to his imprisonment, and with imprisonment, execution, the foreseen conclusion of a way of truth which he declared would make people free. How can my choice of prison, through a deliberate life of resistance bearing that consequence, be understood as a liberating stage of the Way?

Prison is the primary weapon in the State's domestic war. That war begins with the studied manipulation of public opinion against "crime in the streets" to support the sharp buildup of tactical police squads to control insurgency in ghetto areas and counter-culture communities. Riot-control and conspiracy laws are passed as a formal declaration of war against internal enemies: black people who won't wait and young people who won't conform. Once the lawmakers have declared war, the police and the courts wage it with dedication. The purpose of the penal system in that war is to force the State's enemies to their knees. What the American bombing plane is to Indochinese peasants, the threat and use of the penal system is at home to poor, mostly black, Americans: a technique to force subject peoples to remain in colonial roles for an imperialist power. Jacques Ellul's analysis of technique in the modern state, in which means overwhelm ends and any possible human dimension in the name of rational efficiency, has special application to the penal system. Our prisons are techniques for America's violent control of her rebellious poor, and in recent days, increasing numbers of young political resisters. To claim any further purpose for these institutions is, I believe, to dignify them beyond reality. From the experience I have had both within them as a prisoner and visiting others in them, I believe that their clear purpose is raw power in the service of a ruling class.

Today we are all creatures of technique, and it is commonly felt by those in opposition to the State's power that to submit to that power to the extent of becoming a prisoner (through resistance) is to become ineffective in the struggle for change. The way to meet the State's technique, it is argued, is by more effective technique, the way to meet power—greater power. It is obvious that going to prison makes no sense in the struggle for power.

But this kind of opposition to the State's power and technique, while opposed to it in politics (Left versus Right, Cleaver versus Reagan), is in fundamental agreement with its spirit, the spirit of technique. Effectiveness is the determining gauge of value, and it is assumed that everyone knows in general what being effective is and wants to be a part of it—for the sake of the solution. Determine the one best means for each step to power, then make it work. Thus one proceeds through the various grades of political, psychological, and physical force in order to reach a liberating end which becomes less and less visible in the process.

The way of effectiveness runs counter to liberation. To be effective is to be determined in action by a calculated end and means. Thus the philosophy of calculated action, which in the Western world means a pragmatism verging on violence, is our determining factor in making effective decisions. The philosophy of calculation bears with it an assumed relation between the person and his goal of action which is in reality a profound bondage, as Hinduism has taught. In struggling to find and use the one best means or technique, I am so binding myself to a mentally predetermined end that my desire for success, for the fruits of action, is dragging me further and further down into my self. My rationally chosen technique —whether it be the bombing of North Vietnam or the bombing of an ROTC building—compels me into an attitude of self-determined ends which becomes less and less capable of acknowledging the resistance of reality, which will not respond to my techniques by granting me my ends. As frustration mounts, the philosophy of technique will always argue for more forceful means— "escalation"—whose recurring lack of results (toward a dimly remembered value) will deepen my bondage to self and ultimate futility.

Thus the end effect of effectiveness for already established power, in the Pentagon and State Department, is an almost total withdrawal from the real world into a technological game room, a computerized self, whose automated thunder won't work on Vietnamese peasants. But although impotent in their power, the great danger of policy-makers is that their volcanic frustrations will pitch them into the ultimate act of effectiveness, global self-destruction: destroying the world to save it.

The same suicidal effect of technique on self is seen in the revolutionary whose unsuccessful strategies for power are marked by a deepening rhetorical insistence that power be seized, by any means necessary, the means in each case failing more obviously to achieve his objective until his alienation from reality is complete.

Technique is effective in binding the self to itself and away from an engagement with reality. As a means of liberation, the philosophy of technique is, in a literal sense, self-defeating. It is a means of solitary confinement more destructive of a person's freedom than any imprisonment the State can impose.

The Way, however, is not effective. It is free. Jesus lived and died for no self-determined end but to fulfill the Father's will at the center of his being. Gandhi following the teaching of the *Bhagavad-Gita* continually renounced the fruits of his actions, in contrast to his political allies, and remained free of the struggles for power which divided and almost destroyed independent India. The Way is free because it is a way not of technique and self but of openness and Being. The Way of Jesus and Gandhi is the way of liberation because, in being responsive to the suffering and injustice of the human family, it is faithful in every stage of its response to that creative truth of Being which loses its self for the life of all. Being is one. Those who live in its Way are radically free through the gift of themselves in Being's fundamental act of self-emptying love. The Way re-creates in the soul of those who walk it, through the gift of themselves, the union of all creation in the fullness of God. Those who live in the Way are the givers and receivers of freedom because they realize the self-denying, self-fulfilling truth that the purpose of freedom is to create it for others.

Prison as the accepted price of resisting mass murder for the sake of reunion is a liberating stage of the Way because it repudiates in an act of Being the self-confinement of technique which is the most profound form of our common bondage, rulers and resisters alike. The choice of prison as a stage of the Way liberates one from the same bondage of technique and force which is the underlying principle of prison's threat to the self. If that choice of Being by the resister is made deeply and radically enough, the self-confining effect of prison will have been nullified from the beginning by the self-liberating rejection of effectiveness.

The choice of prison through resistance is technically ineffective and spiritually explosive: Gandhi, Bonhoeffer, the Berrigans, and thousands of young American war resisters who by living out their truth behind bars are radically altering lives, their own and others—all speak to the point. If my choice of prison through resistance is to be sustained in me as it has been in others, I must renounce all ends from the beginning (what end can be served by my silence behind bars?) and give myself fully to the silence of a way which offers no guarantees for truth and love. The valley of sun and shadow is a long way from prison, but I believe that prison, like death on a cross, can in faith open a way into a valley of silence where life flows without ceasing.

DEATH AND LIBERATION

Even if I can affirm both my trial and imprisonment in radical freedom, there is one step beyond the solitary confinement of my cell which the Imperial State can take in dealing with my resistance. It can kill me.

Now that *is* far-fetched, isn't it?

Is it?

A certain perspective is helpful here: the real world. In the real world, as opposed to the world of my self:

> Down a creaking, narrow-gauge track, two Indian miners strained to move a rusted cart full of tin ore.
>
> The ore would eventually find its way to Huanuni, in the valley, then to the concentrating mill near Oruro twenty miles away, then to smelters in the United States or Britain, and then, perhaps, to tin cans for the convenience of housewives and, finally, to garbage heaps to be buried again in the earth.
>
> The Indians pushing the cart, whose basic wage is $25 per month, had probably never eaten anything that comes in a tin can. Their cheeks bulged with their staple food—coca leaves, from which cocaine is extracted.
>
> Bolivian miners chew the leaf, which costs five cents for a double handful, because it dampens hunger and gives them energy for work in this thin air.

Behind the one cart, a tiny girl no more than six years old trudged along. Her infant brother peered out from the tattered shawl that held him to his sister's back. The little girl's feet were bound in mud-caked rags. Her legs were blue.

She was looking along the track for pieces of ore shaken loose from the carts. If the ore is of high grade, it can be exchanged for food in illicit stores. (A news story from Bolivia; New York *Times*, August 25, 1967)

In the real world, as opposed to the world of my self, there are several hundred million little girls and baby brothers and destitute parents whom the Imperial State's system of wealth and power feeds upon daily. In the real world, as opposed to the world of my self, these millions of people, principally in Latin America, Asia, and Africa, who are the unseen victims of our political distribution of the world's goods, know at close range what an impact of death the American way of life brings.

Granted those people are poor and starving (we all know that), there's no reason for seeing an American conspiracy behind it.

Not an American conspiracy. No U.S. board of directors ever sat down to design gas chambers for Latin American peasants. It just happens that the political and economic system which developed out of apparently innocent U.S. board meetings is reaping its wealth in death in the not-so-far corners of the world.

Be specific.

Prior to the Cuban Revolution and in cooperation with Batista, the United States controlled 80% of Cuban utilities, 90% of Cuban mines, 90% of Cuban cattle ranches, almost 100% of Cuban oil refineries, 50% of Cuban public railways, 40% of the Cuban sugar industry, 25% of Cuban bank balances. Because men and women gave their lives in a revolution, the Cuban people now share those resources. But the situation of United States control of other people's resources hasn't changed in most of the world, where forty countries have an average per capita income of less than $120 a year while foreign corporations extract huge amounts of wealth from their land and forests. That is the real world, the world which delivers canned goods to the American supermarket, which latter is the air-conditioned world of your and my self.

The Imperial State with its economic system kills millions in the real world and, with the greatest military power in history, it shoots and bombs those who challenge its control. In the world of my self, I feel none of that power. Even as trial and prison bring me out of my self into the real world, still with my white American middle-class background I feel relatively little of the power of the Imperial State, which is concentrated on the back of the Bolivian tin miner and on men such as Che Guevara who respond to him. But the fearful truth is that, wherever I am in my life, I can *always* travel a deeper way of liberation into the real world. The question of the Imperial State's attitude toward my life and death in this world will always be a relative one: Just how far do I want to go in?

I dreamed I was walking along the highway in the valley where I was born. It was soon after dawn, when the white light spreading out from the mountains passed into one's body. Dawning light reaching into my bones. The valley was quiet, only the soft sound of my footsteps. The fields and trees were still. There was smoke up ahead across the highway. A drift of it curled silently into the sky. I walked on, approaching the bank of smoke.

The smoke, nearer now and beginning to envelop me, made me more conscious of the stillness of the valley. I looked up, saw the silent white light of the sky disappearing in the haze. I stopped. A void opened inside me. The valley ahead was thick with the smell of burning. This way would mean someone's life. But as I turned in my dream, there was nothing behind me except an even thicker smoke—no way back, no glimpse of the morning light, nothing. The way of the valley lay ahead and could be rediscovered only in the midst of smoke and fire.

Evil in the world is a mystery which we enter. It defies our efforts to explain its presence, or our presence in it. The truth of our response to evil lies not in explanation but in life, in our resistance to it, which involves us further in the mystery and in death.

The decision to resist evil's social forms with love and truth—thus to resist through non-resistance—is a decision to enter a dark night of the soul and of the world. Resistance is a decision to struggle with the powers of darkness: the kind of power which pressed down upon the world during the days and nights of the Cuban missile crisis, the tensely waiting power which lay over Dallas while John Kennedy waved to the crowd from his back seat, the power of darkness which one felt in the streets of Chicago as helmets and night sticks moved forward, the darkness which fills brightly lit rooms where policy-makers lean over maps and peoples, the power of darkness in myself when moved to destroy all that (and them). Resistance enters into the mystery of this power, meets it with truth, and overcomes one stage of darkness in the process of giving a life. For the price of truth and love in resistance to the mystery of evil, in its depths of darkness, is the life of the resister. There are depths of encountering evil with good from which one cannot return: Gandhi, Martin King, Malcolm X, Robert Kennedy, died less from the bullets of assassins than they did from entering that inner chamber of men's hearts in which hate and death are tangible, to say with love to those powers of destruction, "It's over now. We've seen the final vision and you're not part of it." Darkness at the prospect of its own death winces and falls back, but not until after lashing out, and the cost of the encounter is the prophet's death.

In choosing resistance I must choose my own death, whether or not it is ever in fact demanded in that struggle with the powers of darkness. If my resistance is real, it must continue to go into reality, meeting and engaging the powers on ever deeper levels, uncovering new dimensions of evil and responsibility for change—eventually touching, circling, risking the possibility of my own death in an ultimate encounter of truth.

But here the mystery of evil engages my self in turn on the level of complete co-responsibility. As much as I would wish it so, the mystery of evil—which with deeper penetration becomes the mystery of death, humanity's and my own—can never be external to myself. Evil is in fact my self, as it is every man's self, a life-divisive self. Evil is recognizable in action as the less-than-whole, self-divided choices of men. Evil is the will's divisive choice of part of the whole: the choice of America before the world, the choice of a party before a people, the choice of self-interest before community, my choice of this without looking at that (which if seen and affirmed, I know yet do not wish to know, would take me out of evil into wholeness). Evil is often done out of what we feel to be duty, especially in high places, but it is always a duty to self—duty to national honor, to party, to my own best interests. Evil is the self's division of the whole, a life-destructive (because wholly disruptive) act which the self defends as necessary to itself, which in fact it is. Because evil radically divides and destroys, it anticipates death as its natural culmination in man's final division.

The deeper my resistance to a social evil goes, the more evident it becomes how inadequate all direct action is, for the source of evil has become more and more closely identified with myself. What I am resisting, which began as a clearly defined imperialism (and which, in terms of political analysis, may remain so to the end), emerges with sharper clarity as my own inner imperialism toward every member of the human family.

The truth comes home to me in a friend's description of Simone Weil: "She only felt at ease on the lowest rung of the social ladder, lost among the masses of poor folk and outcasts of this world." Simone Weil felt the world truly, and thus identified her life spiritually and materially with the poorest of her world—to the point of an early death through malnutrition, which in her radically Gospel view was a normal and just conclusion of life.

The point here is not only that I do not act as Simone Weil in her living and dying identification with the world's poor, but that I hardly begin to feel as she did in response to exploited and suffering people. It is true that if I both felt and acted wholly according to this radically Gospel view, which even Simone Weil did not do (and suffered deeply from that self-knowledge), I could no more survive the conditions of this earth than can the poorest scavenger in Calcutta. But it is equally true that my failure to correspond—and my failure no small one—to the living demands of love from my poorest brothers and sisters convicts me in conscience and act of the very same imperialism of which I indict my society. What I deserve, from the standpoint of both a just and knowing God and the poorest of peoples, in this world of injustice which I feed upon, is death—and that same death, by the mystery of evil which thus engages my self (as I engage it) in co-responsibility, is what I will inevitably, and justifiably, experience. Death comes, then, as the just conclusion of the life of mutual exploitation in which all humanity shares (even the poorest feed on one another), and I in a special degree.

Moreover, this exploitation of which I am guilty reaches from the most afflicted poor of the human family (in the political and economic realities of daily living) back to the exploitation (in more personal ways) of those nearest in love, in our own home. Subtle forms of coercion, power instead of love, become expedient means of dealing with, rather than encountering, my own flesh: Shelley, our children; nearest, most painful victims of my inner imperialism. With its cover now finally ripped off, my own imperialism is seen to have caused pain and death in a karma I cannot trace, from near to far members of the human family.

What began therefore in my resistance as a rebellion against exploitation becomes a humbling process of recognizing its pervasive presence in myself to the point of a justly suffered death. To resist and encounter truly the powers becomes a process of acknowledging that *I* am a major source of their power to kill others.

At the same time this acknowledgment of evil's source in my self cannot cease to coincide with a yet deeper engagement on the level of social conflict: Imperialism, war, racism are no less intolerable as institutions because of my guilt, no less visible in their domination over people's lives, and the need to identify and denounce their specifically institutional forms when I see these forms reflected in myself, is, if anything, greater—to the discomfort of both society and my own life as a consequence. It has simply become obvious in this process of engaging evil in society for the sake of a redeeming truth—a more loving, more human community—just how profound my co-responsibility for this evil lies.

But for resistance to survive long and fruitfully this deepening awareness of my own guilt, it will have to experience an infinitely forgiving Love and undergo the purifying fire of its own self-giving. Only the liberating gift of Love to me and of my self to Love in return can sustain me in resisting truly an imperialism whose heightened identification with myself in conscience will otherwise force me into self-hatred or self-righteousness, the dangers of the maturing Marxist. Self-emptying love for others—*all* the others, from those nearest in love, to the most afflicted poor and their exploiters (whom others exploit)—is the radically liberating reality capable of supporting resistance beyond an adolescent awareness of self. A life of love discovered and founded on the gift of Love is the final form of the Way. Love liberates me from evil's source of division in my self and makes me whole in a greater Reality. So as resistance increases (while love deepens) to the point of risking my life in the struggle for truth, I must welcome that risk because only to the extent that my life has become a more and more complete gift of my self can I remain true to the struggle as I perceive it in its inner dimension.

Thus death enters life not as intruder and threat but as the liberating way itself, as a way of giving, once death has revealed its face in resistance and contemplation as my potentially life-affirming end through a final gift of self back to the Love which gave me life. Death as the gift of self in and to Love is the ultimately liberating act which overcomes evil and makes life wholly and finally affirmative.

Death seen thus as gift and freely accepted end enters into life. Death accepted in Love gives its life to a progressive dying to self made up of immeasurable small actions, experiments in truth, which in their acknowledgment of the absolute void within me constitute the basis for an ongoing resistance to totalitarian power in the world. Evil is resisted and overcome by a force of truth whose infinite possibility, the God of history, depends on the progressive reduction of my self to zero. Man is liberated in Love by a naked acceptance of death on a cross.

This valley is empty like the soul of Jesus on the cross. I begin to understand its liberating power in this emptiness, a way of life in which the silence of a void is the beginning of all understanding and power.

On a dark night Jesus cried out in the center of his valley, "My God, my God, why have you forsaken me?" The void answered with silence. Yet the dark silence, like that of Gethsemane, was the most liberating answer possible, for it emptied Jesus of any conceivable claim to power, rendered him the most powerless of creatures, handed his life over completely to the Father: "Father, into your hands I commit my spirit." On the cross Jesus experienced a valley whose emptiness was total, thus freeing him for his total gift of life in death to the Father.

Resistance with its consequences of trial, imprisonment, and death is meant to empty me of self and liberate a new man in the world, no longer subject to the powers of darkness—so that the inner way of the valley can be a purifying fire for the revolution and the building of the kingdom, a power for the liberation of humanity and the creation of a new world beyond imperialism, war, and racism.

With the smoke blown away, dispersed in the dawning white light of the valley, there is a man walking beside me on the highway.

I can't remember . . . Your name is . . .

Black.

Vietnamese.

Chicano.

Bolivian.

Cuban.

Indian.

Pakistani.

Bengali.

Chinese.

Arab.

Israeli.

Russian.

Brother.

The man has become a great crowd of people who fan out from the highway and stretch across the valley, walking through the fields which are rippled by a morning breeze and pass from white to gold under the changing color of the sky. The people are singing. There have never been so many people in the valley, never so much joy to break the silence with singing and laughter which reach up the rock walls and cliffs to that tree-lined ridge in the East where the valley's day begins. The sun is up. We are a new people. Join us.